CW01646810

‘A starting point for anyone i abolition.’
— *gal-dem*

‘*Brick by Brick* is devoted to dismantling and rebuilding ... Cradle advocate a revolutionary, compassionate communalism: “We must commit to care by any and all means necessary.”’
— *The New Statesman*

‘[An] important contribution to the conversation on the steps needed to begin the journey [to abolition].’
— *Labour Hub*

‘A warm invitation into critical thinking that elucidates the carceral landscape of the UK and clarifies what must be done to end it. When Cradle write, they are speaking to you and me about our responsibilities to one another and to building a world that is *life-affirming*. On every page, their political determination is laid bare; they implore their readers to understand that our resistance must be tenacious, organised and strategic. But it must also be infused with a revolutionary love—they show us how we can make this world anew.’
— Lola Olufemi, author of *Experiments in Imagining Otherwise* and *Feminism, Interrupted*

‘An unflinching account of everyday injustices; a practical workbook; a manifesto for how we are all called to do the life-affirming work of abolition—this book is an unmissable call to care, to imagine and to build the world we need.’
— Joshua Virasami, author of *How to Change It*

‘Cradle shows us that abolition is—irresistibly!—a doing word. This is the work: lives lived in collective social practice, always already in translation, wayfinding, toward a new and abundant world. Across geography and generation, let us meet in the flower gardens of liberation study—let us bloom!’
— Imani Robinson, writer and curator

'This brilliant and necessary book embodies the joy, radical optimism, uncertainty, care-fullness and urgency of abolition! Cradle rigorously guides us through the connections between the harm we see around us and the ways we are always already resisting it, revealing how very present and possible it is to build a new world of justice.'
— Suhaiymah Manzoor-Khan, author of *Tangled in Terror* and *Postcolonial Banter*

'*Brick by Brick* provides a devastating account of the UK's prison industrial complex, but it also celebrates the motley crew of organisers working right now to dismantle it. Highlighting the power of care, imagination and resistance in our movements, this book is absolutely indispensable. Read it, now!'
— Luke de Noronha, author of *Deporting Black Britons*

'This is the book that UK abolitionists have been waiting for—collaborative, accessible, pragmatic, community-centred and clear-sighted. It broadens and deepens our understanding of the societal bricks that do not keep us safe or free, and it points us to abolitionist theory in practice, from the grassroots. Thank you, Cradle Community, for this irresistible invitation to dismantle, to resist and to build a world in which no one is left out.'
— Zahra Bei, No More Exclusions

'A much-needed resource for readers in the UK who imagine building a safer world. Accessible, thorough and urgent—a must-read!'
— Travis Alabanza, writer, performer and theatre maker

'It is so vital to have a book that focuses on carceral structures here in the UK, and keeps an abolitionist focus firmly on prisons, their ideological support, and what to do about it.'
— Sami Çapulcu, *Act Build Change* blog

'A germinal handbook for those in the UK and beyond, *Brick by Brick* offers fierce tools, maps and provocations for our collective liberation. Centring the labour of abolitionist feminists, Cradle has produced a powerful and resourceful intervention. Study, discuss and engage!'
— Erica R. Meiners, co-author of *The Feminist and the Sex Offender* and *Flaunt It!*

BRICK BY BRICK

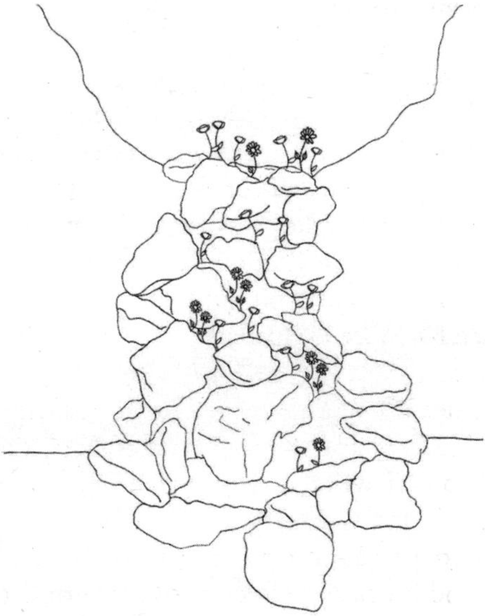

First edition published in 2021
Second edition published in 2023
by Hajar Press C.I.C., London, United Kingdom
www.hajarpress.com
@hajarpress

© Cradle Community, 2021

The right of Cradle Community to be identified as the author of this work has been asserted by them in accordance with the Copyright, Designs and Patents Act, 1988.

All rights reserved. No part of this publication may be reproduced, distributed or transmitted, in any form or by any means, without the written permission of the publisher.

ISBN 978-1-914221-28-6 Paperback
ISBN 978-1-914221-29-3 EPUB eBook

A Cataloguing-in-Publication data record for this book is available from the British Library.

Cover and interior art: Han Gunji Stephens
Cover design: Samara Jundi
Typesetting: Laura Jones / lauraflojo.com

Printed and bound in the United Kingdom by
Clays Ltd, Elcograf S.p.A.

BRICK BY BRICK

How We Build a World Without Prisons

CRADLE COMMUNITY

Contents

PREFACE TO THE SECOND EDITION

REVOLUTION IS STILL AN EMERGENCY

Writing this book during Covid lockdowns meant that Cradle had to lean into uncertainty and act with hope. Every day, it felt like anything could happen. Now, amidst the collapse, our ideas don't seem so impossible or utopian anymore. Where more people than ever are looking for transformation, abolitionists are offering a path through. We are in a state of chaos, standing in the gap between what is and what could be, gathering and distributing the resources we need through mutual aid and radical love to fill the void left by white-supremacist capitalism.

Since *Brick by Brick* was first published in 2021, politics in the UK has continued to downslide towards fascism. The Police, Crime, Sentencing and Courts Act 2022 has given even more power to the police to repress protest, and the government is pushing its plan through the courts to deport migrants to Rwanda. There are more police patrolling schools, and we are witnessing rising transphobic violence. In a renewed era of Tory austerity, working people are struggling to survive what has been dubbed a 'cost-of-living crisis', facing huge rises in the prices of food, necessities and energy, all while fossil fuel companies and other mega-corporations continue banking multi-billion-pound profits and the military industrial complex runs into overdrive. The Labour Party refuses to read the room, doubling down on its 'tough on crime' approach with a promise to put 13,000 more police officers on the streets if elected.

At the same time, the last few years have seen resistance, political education and campaigns against policing and prisons continue to grow. The murder of Chris Kaba, a twenty-four-year-old Black man shot dead by the Metropolitan Police in 2022, sparked nationwide protests. Local copwatch groups have spread across the UK, leading trainings so that people know how to intervene when they witness policing in their neighbourhoods. More and more stories of sexual and domestic violence by police officers have come out in the two years since Sarah Everard's murder, causing trust in the police, particularly by women, to plummet, so that even mainstream media has been pushed to acknowledge the shift in public perception. When 'protecting women's safety' has been the justification for so much policing, this rise in general awareness is vital for building resistance.

For Cradle, these years have brought a lot of pain and stress to the surface. We have lost friends and family members. Since this book's first release, at least four people have died in a single women's prison, HMP Eastwood Park, including a beloved comrade, Taylor. State violence is relentless. Through our grief, whilst tending to our feelings, we are conscious to constantly remind ourselves of why we organise against violence—not in the interest of revenge but for the sake of caring for each other. The state does not care for us or keep us safe. Revolution is still an emergency.

Each of our lives has changed a lot since we wrote the book, but our core beliefs—in the importance of community and solidarity, and that a just world is possible—continue to guide what we do. Our collective has spread out, and we are now living across the UK, Turtle Island/North America and Germany, with strengthened connections to the Caribbean. We've each been focusing on building community where we are physically, and it's been beautiful to lean on our relationships with each other as we do this. We've been exploring creative and joyful projects, connecting with our traditional spiritual practices, DJing, writing and spinning basketballs on the court.

Wherever we are, we've all been thinking about the skills and resources we're going to recycle to build a world without prisons. We want to experiment as much as we can at the local level. Some of us are organising against policing, some engaged in community initiatives to build relationships, and some disrupting violence between young people. Our ideas about how to respond to violence and protect each other from harm are ever evolving, and we continue to have fruitful conversations about transformative justice. We have faced confronting and heart-breaking challenges and conflicts, as well as absorbed the lessons they have taught us about practising community accountability.

Working on this book through lockdowns taught us the importance of self-accountability, being honest, and communicating our limits and needs to each other. We only made it because of our commitment to working slowly, paying careful attention, and affirming each other's humanity. Sacrificing ourselves or our relationships, rushing to complete this work, or insisting on its perfection would not have been in alignment with the abolitionist principles we hold. If we could add to what we have written in this book, it would be to more explicitly outline the intertwined mechanisms of white supremacy and fascism as driving forces of political repression in Britain, and to highlight more examples of anti-imperialist struggles and non-carceral approaches to violence from the Global South, which we are still connecting with and learning from. We would also have loved to write about how to engage in spirituality through ancestral practices in ways that have not been co-opted by white supremacy and capitalism (where are your crystals or your white sage coming from?), honouring our connections to each other and our environment. Much more could have been explored, but *Brick by Brick* is only a beginning.

Writing this book collectively has been an incredible opportunity to build each other up and celebrate our bravery and wins when we work together. In the time since publication, we have held and been held in some beautiful online and offline spaces, connecting with specific communities to talk about abolition, and each one has been really special. Importantly, people have taken the book on as the resource we wrote it to be, starting reading groups and discussion spaces of their own and sharing the text with youth groups, squats, schools and libraries. We are so grateful for the love and positivity we have received as a collective about this work, especially from young people, incarcerated people and new organisers. Hearing that this book has become an intro to abolition in the British context is all we hoped for.

We hope *Brick by Brick* can be a practical offering towards meeting the growing public desire for alternatives. We hope it inspires readers to connect and take action in line with abolitionist principles in their daily lives, such as teachers and healthcare workers coming together in their mass refusal to be treated as disposable in the face of public health crises, transport workers acting in solidarity with passengers protesting fare hikes, and anyone refusing to report people under oppressive immigration policies and PREVENT legislation. We hope reading the book creates space to take pause together. We hope it encourages more people to join in building community-led responses to increasingly hostile conditions. We hope its examples and insights disrupt nostalgia for a pre-Covid past and instead motivate us to pay attention to what we can learn from the pandemic about accessibility and practices of care.

Most of all, we hope readers come away from this book with our feeling of hope that the world does not have to hurt like this, and that we can organise to transform it together, brick by brick.

PLAYLIST

Nas feat. Lauryn Hill – 'If I Ruled the World (Imagine That)'

Ruby Ibarra feat. Rocky Rivera, Klassy & Faith Santilla – 'Us'

Ana Tijoux – 'Antifa Dance'

Lowkey – 'Long Live Palestine'

Nina Simone – 'Backlash Blues'

Jamila Woods feat. Nico Segal – 'BALDWIN'

SAULT – 'Wildfires'

Fela Kuti – 'Water No Get Enemy'

Nailah Blackman x Sammy Jo – 'Farmer'

Sampa the Great feat. Zaachariaha – 'Healer'

Toots and the Maytals – 'Time Tough'

RAY BLK feat. Stormzy – 'My Hood'

Manga Saint Hilare & Murkage Dave – 'We Need to Look After Us (Pt. 2)'

Tiggs Da Author – 'Blame It on the Youts'

Dolly Parton – '9 to 5'

Lauryn Hill – 'Everything Is Everything'

Tems – 'Free Mind'

Ric Wilson – 'Fight Like Ida B & Marsha P'

Kash Doll – '100 of Us'

Bellah – 'Evil Eye'

Kelela – 'Altadena'

Leven Kali – 'Joy'

Mahalia – 'Never Change'

ENNY feat. Amia Brave – 'Peng Black Girls'

Patrice Roberts – 'Better Days'

NOTE ON LANGUAGE

We are in a constant state of reflection around our use of language. In this book, we talk about a range of interactions from interpersonal conflict and domestic and sexual violence to state violence, all of which are varied and all of which cause harm. By harm, we are referring to acts and conditions that cause pain, suffering and negative mental, emotional and physical impact. While some harms are felt momentarily and can be easily repaired, others are life-altering and long lasting; many more fall somewhere in between.

We don't refer to people as criminals, inmates, convicts or offenders in our narrative, nor do we define them by the harms they have caused. We instead honour the humanity of people who are criminalised, using terms like people in prison, people inside, incarcerated people and people who have caused harm. However, we do not do the same for police officers, immigration officers or prison guards, as these are positions of power conferred by violent institutions.

We understand that the state violently imposes the gender binary on us, and not everyone in a women's prison identifies as a woman, nor everyone in a men's prison as a man. We therefore try to refer to how the state labels such institutions without labelling the people inside them. Statistics, unfortunately, are often not so nuanced.

We recognise the work of Indigenous organisers in settler colonies from whom we've learned the importance of using the Indigenous names for different regions. Based on our (hoped-for) readership in the UK, we expect that a lot of readers will not immediately be familiar with all of these names, as a result of the deep whitewashing in Western history and geography. We include the Indigenous names of certain places in brackets so as to begin to bridge the gap of unfamiliarity while bringing these names into more common usage, and we recognise the ongoing violence of settler colonialism.

Language changes and evolves quickly, and so we expect that some words that we use here, such as people of colour, might become outdated soon. We're excited to see our language and ideas grow together with you, and for the diving board that is this book to send ripples of conversation and critique out across our communities.

OUR FOUNDATIONS, OUR CO-CONSPIRATORS, OUR GUIDES

Our work as Cradle Community has focused on creating temporary spaces for learning, joy and solidarity, whether through transformative justice workshops or our Freedom Fighters Feast dinner events. We and our loved ones live under threat of violence, which manifests at home, school and university, in relationships and on the street, through housing precarity, police, psychiatrists and borders. We commit to abolitionist politics every day by supporting the people close to us in their struggles against state, domestic and sexual violence with whatever we can offer. We have connected with other abolitionists and transformative justice practitioners across the world and learned so much from them and their work. It has been an honour to collaborate with so many of these people for this book.

Our foundational references for this work are both individuals and collectives, of whom three of the most influential are Claudia Jones, Mia Mingus and Sisters Uncut.

Claudia Jones was a Trinidadian communist, feminist and later Pan-Africanist, who was imprisoned in New York and deported to Trinidad before moving to London. Her activism and writing about the 'superexploitation'—oppression through class, race and gender—of Black women and her commitment to working within marginalised communities in London were important in building collective power across internationalist anti-racist struggles. The founder of Notting Hill Carnival and of the *West Indian Gazette*, she was such a threat to the existing power structure that she was surveilled by the FBI until she died. Oppressed people have continued to develop and explore the ideologies of Pan-Africanism, socialism and anti-imperialism. We join in this important work.

Mia Mingus is a transformative justice practitioner and disability justice organiser in the Bay Area, San Francisco (occupied land of the Ohlone people), whose work and wisdom as an individual and with the Bay Area Transformative Justice Collective has taught us so much about how to bring discussions of transformative justice and community accountability into our everyday lives. Her ideas help us to appreciate the deep reflective work that it takes to be in community with each other and the importance of building our skills in working through conflict and violence towards collective transformation.

Founded in London in 2014, Sisters Uncut is an abolitionist feminist direct action group of women and gender-non-conforming people fighting against dangerous austerity cuts to state support for survivors of domestic and sexual violence. From dyeing the fountains in Trafalgar Square red to symbolise the blood on the government's hands, to gate-crashing the red carpet at the BAFTAs in protest of the criminalisation of survivors, to political occupations of council flats and Holloway Prison, the work of Sisters Uncut has been fundamental not only to our own journey as organisers, but also to the growing abolitionist feminist movement in the UK. Sisters Uncut taught us the power of sharp political analysis turned into action and about the collective reflection needed to sustain a caring community.

We write in gratitude to the work of so many others, including Fred Moten, Mariame Kaba, Beth Richie, Ruth Wilson Gilmore, Dorothy Roberts, Leah Lakshmi Piepzna-Samarasinha, Mimi Kim, Olive Morris, Generation Five, INCITE!, Survived and Punished, Paul Kahawatte and Navigate, Bryony Beynon, and the many anonymous transformative justice practitioners who do amazing work and have been building alternatives to prison and punishment for years. We are grateful for all of our friends, chosen family and co-conspirators who have had those late-night chats with us about safety and freedom. We write with thanks to the great voices of the Black feminist tradition, including Stella Dadzie, Professor Diana Paton, bell hooks and Audre Lorde, who have helped us to reimagine anti-violence work; to Angela Davis and Critical Resistance, who gave us language for prison abolition; to Assata Shakur and her fight for socialism and Black revolution; to the Combahee River Collective for their contributions on identity politics and the practice of radical solidarity; to A. Sivanandan, Andaiye and Walter Rodney for their teachings on international solidarity; and to all communities around the world united in resistance against colonialism. Lastly, we thank our wonderful editors and publishers, Farhaana Arefin and Brekhna Aftab, who have supported us in putting together this book with positivity and grace. Thank you for believing in this project.

Our collective is dedicated to building: building radical spaces; building our expertise in intervening in and de-escalating violence; building frameworks to reimagine how we understand health and wellbeing; building strong bases of support and care for survivors; and building new approaches to accountability in our work with people who have caused serious harm. Through our experiences of violence and oppression driven by constructs of gender, race, class, sexuality and disability, through studying the work of radical organisers and scholars, and through simply getting stuck into the work of community care, we hope to offer useful insights while understanding that we will continue to learn. Although we have all brought our individual experiences to the creation of this book, we have written this as a collective in acknowledgement that individual acclaim is counter to our message, and because none of us could do this alone.

Our political principles are collectivity; dismantling white-supremacist structural power; dismantling imperial and neo-colonial power; developing inclusive people power; and redistributing resources towards community care and self-determination. We follow in the tradition of Black feminists, Black radicals and anti-capitalists in the Global South in their explorations of what liberation really looks like. We acknowledge that many of our influences and forerunners began with a Marxist class analysis, which they developed to incorporate anti-colonial and feminist dimensions. Similarly, the long legacy of anarchist organising in the UK informs the radical history of labour that many of us engage with. We share in these organisers' critique of the abuse enabled by centralised power (the state), but like Claudia Jones, we are 'left of Marx'—we are explicitly working to build a world without prisons or white supremacy.

This is our offering to others who are trying to build an alternative to the violence of the British police and prison system. It is for those who feel the acute tightness of disempowerment in their chest but who want to fight—to take action from the UK as part of the global abolitionist project. Written in 2020–2021, this book is a snapshot of our research into how folks across the UK are dismantling the current system and building new abolitionist realities.

INTRODUCTION

A world without prisons is nothing like the world we live in now. It is a world built on collective safety and care—for all of us. To build such a world, it is essential that we abolish the prison system and every structure that serves to deprive us of our freedom, safety and dignity. The global prison abolitionist movement resists all forms of violence and oppression, inviting us to work to transform our relationships with each other and with the Earth.

We are living through a cycle—of witnessing police violence, either in person or online, followed by public outrage and pain, followed by ineffective reform, followed by more police violence.

Throughout the 1960s and '70s, demands made by Black liberation movements—to free the people and invest in communities—resonated with oppressed people fighting capitalism and empire around the world. They almost won. But many revolutionary leaders across the globe were imprisoned and murdered, often through the collaboration of anti-communist Western states, keen to control the Global South in the post-independence era. In 2002, the Belgian government finally apologised for its role in the assassination of Pan-Africanist Patrice Lumumba, the first president of what is now the Democratic Republic of Congo, in 1961. The assassination of revolutionary Walter Rodney in Georgetown, Guyana in 1980 is still a 'mystery'. The memories of these movements were often buried along with them.

Since the early 2010s, police and state brutality in Britain and the United States has sparked huge protest movements against state violence, from the murder of Mark Duggan by the Metropolitan Police, which led to the London riots in 2011, to the rise of the Black Lives Matter (BLM) movement in the USA. More recently, the murders by US police of George Floyd and Breonna Taylor led to another wave of global BLM protests in the summer of 2020. Coupled with decades of austerity and attacks on public services, these events gave rise to mass calls to defund the police and abolish prisons altogether. Politicians openly scoffed at these demands or weakly attempted to co-opt them, and corporations hurriedly sought to placate us with vague promises about racial equity in empty public statements. Simultaneously, we have been living through the widest, most comprehensive and most invasive expansion of the criminal justice system in decades. Revolution is an emergency. We have to continue to move forward together with clear intention and vigilance.

In Britain, we are taught from a young age to outsource our problems with each other to teachers, social workers, the council or the police. We are taught that punishment, exclusion and shame are inevitable parts of conflict; that there are good people and bad people, and that everyone risks becoming disposable if they don't conform. Austerity's attack on youth centres and community centres in the UK, as well as the heightened policing of unused property, has led to a severe lack of space to gather and so build solidarity and comradery, or to address conflict. What does it mean politically to call to move resources from the police to communities, when austerity cuts have already been defunding the police, and in response the British Labour Party has been pushing a pro-police narrative against Conservative cuts? Against this backdrop, we hold on to abolition as a path that maps out our revolution beyond the limitations and frustrations of electoral politics.

The work of academics Akwugo Emejulu and Leah Bassel demonstrates how for many women of colour, that devastation, that lack of support, was a reality before Tory austerity and a fact of life under a white-supremacist, patriarchal status quo. For decades, community groups made up of radical Black and brown working-class people have been undermined and disrupted by the state. Black communities, migrant communities and the working classes—and within these communities those of us who are disabled and/or queer—have long known that police and the institutions they uphold don't protect us and were never designed to. We've had to create our own ways of supporting ourselves when our government refuses to do so, or actively tries to destroy us. We have always had to rely on each other.

The truth about the prison industrial complex is that its current structures—prisons, detention centres, borders—are pretty new social institutions in human history. They have not always existed, and they will not always exist. But as with every resilient structure for authoritarian control, in the centuries since it first developed, the so-called criminal justice system has evolved and undergone numerous reforms across the world. We reject the notion that reforms—which always serve and strengthen the prison industrial complex—can deliver justice, since we believe that keeping human beings in cages is not justice. We know, both from experience and statistical data, that punishment does not work to provide safety or deter harmful behaviour, and we know that this is not a failure of the system but a product of its design.

We follow in the legacy of the Combahee River Collective in our recognition that to be at the centre of the most important struggles for liberation is to align yourself with those on the margins of society. No one is pushed further out of sight and out of mind than those in prison, as society attempts to vanish them altogether. The prison is at the centre of modern-day oppression. Punishment and exploitation are prioritised over public health. Abolition calls for a revolution—in care, safety and wellbeing.

In order to abolish criminal justice and live the politics of transformative justice, we must reorient the way we understand central questions and concepts. What is violence? Who is a 'criminal'? What do prisons, police, courts and the other elements of the prison industrial complex claim to do, and what is their true purpose?

Reframing crime, violence and safety

Crime is a distraction—the framing of public safety as a battle between 'good' cops and 'bad' criminals masks the harms enforced and perpetuated by the state. Keeping anyone in a cage is a violent response to violence, and while prisons are disguised as being necessary for public safety, they are themselves inherently unsafe. We can thus see that not everything that hurts us is classed as a crime, while not everything that is a crime causes harm to people. We also know that people who have access to power and money do not live under the same laws as people who don't.

Sex work, drug possession and not paying your TV licence are all crimes worthy of state punishment. Yet the deaths of seventy-two people in the Grenfell Tower fire, state-sanctioned killing during war, healthcare cuts, preventable deaths in care homes from Covid-19, and evictions of people from their homes are not deemed criminal. This reveals the truth that criminal law is designed not to keep us safe and prevent harm, but rather to control and punish those made vulnerable by the state through poverty, addiction, homelessness, illness, xenophobia, patriarchy, racism, queerphobia, transphobia and ableism. Our government does not tackle the social isolation and conditions of deprivation that lead to further harm; instead, it cracks down on those it labels as 'criminals'. Crime is a construct that changes depending on its targets, applied to some but never to others.

In thinking about our safety, we refuse to ignore those endangered by the state's violence. We also expand our understanding of violence beyond the physical to encompass the emotional and mental control exerted by those with systemically conferred—a power dynamic exploited by the state. Violence, then, is not just between individuals; it is structural.

But what about the rapists/murderers?

Contrary to how abolition may be portrayed in the press, prioritising the safety of children, women, trans people and gender-non-conforming people is at the centre of everything we do. We are sick of rape and violence being treated as an inevitable part of the human experience. We reject the idea that the root cause of these harms is the existence of innately bad people ('rapists and murderers') in our societies, as well as the myth that the criminal justice system and prison industrial complex protect people from sexual violence and murder. In fact, people die every year in state custody, invasive body searches are commonplace, and coercion and violence run rampant. In a safe society, state officials should not be able to sexually assault you for a pay cheque, inside or outside of prison walls.

Prison doesn't do anything to prevent rape or murder, and the police are useless at intervening in instances of stalking and domestic abuse. Hundreds of accusations of domestic abuse are made against police officers themselves every year. Meanwhile, many members of the public, such as sex workers and undocumented people, are unable to report the violence they're subjected to at the hands of the police, but this violence nevertheless exists.

In short, the system we have clearly isn't working—we can't rely on a system that is itself harmful to protect us from harm. Instead, we must ask: What is our society doing right now to prevent murder and assault? How do we eliminate these harms, rather than treating them as an inevitability?

When someone is violent towards another person, what are our priorities: safety, or punishment? Rather than viewing rape and murder as random acts by individual monsters, it can help us to find a way out if we recognise abuse and violence as part of a wider culture of dominance and control. This way, we can challenge and change the structures that produce harm in the first place.

If you're not convinced yet, that's okay. If you stick with us, we ask you to consider this question as you go on: Is the punishment of a tiny proportion of those in our society who rape and kill, after the fact, enough to justify the expansive, ongoing use of violence, control and surveillance that we lay out in this book? Can't we do better?

About this book

Brick by Brick is based on conversations we have had within the abolitionist movement, especially among people with whom we have built relationships. Due to the material risks of speaking out from inside prison, or of putting your name to this radical work, some contributors are anonymous.

In the following work, we outline the bricks that need to be torn down in order to transform the conditions under which we live for the better. First, we demonstrate how ideas of criminality and punishment affect and are ingrained in many aspects of our lives, from our historical context, to the food we eat, to the entertainment we consume, to the gender binary, to the state's provision of housing, education and care. Each of these sites of oppression and punishment is also a site of resistance. The second section of the book is a vision for what an abolitionist approach could look like, highlighting the radically inclusive and collaborative systems we are assembling to build a safer world.

Abolition asks for more than just demolition of buildings. It asks for the complete dismantling of the world as we know it and the building of a whole new one, which will offer such an abundance of care that there will be no space in our minds, let alone in our communities, for things like prisons. This work is an experiment in connecting the dots—an exploration of how we can honour centuries of resistance and respond to the new challenges of our generation.

We reject the myth that imprisonment, surveillance and control keep us safe or solve social and economic problems. Abolition is the work of creating a world full of love, health, education, food, shared abundance, dignity, safety, justice and freedom. To realise this world, we must tear down, transform and rebuild the very bricks of our lives.

1.

THE CRIMINAL JUSTICE SYSTEM

Britain's massive prison population is sustained through the targeted criminalisation of people committing acts of survival, in one way or another, whether that be theft, handling stolen goods, drug-related offences or sex work. According to the 2021 'Bromley Briefings Prison Factfile' by the Prison Reform Trust, more than two thirds of people in prison were unemployed in the month before being taken into custody, and 15% were homeless. Many of the people in women's prisons convicted of murder are known even by the justice system to have been defending themselves against someone who had been abusing them, often for years, and almost a third of people in women's prisons are convicted simply for not paying their TV licence fee. This is not to make the argument that the state should be putting the 'right' people in prison, but rather to highlight how those struggling to survive are systematically criminalised.

While the state labels some people as 'violent offenders' and others as 'non-violent offenders', we know that its judgement of who is violent is unreliable and racist. And while it's true that on rare occasions some people do commit extreme acts of violence, incarceration has not been shown to reduce that kind of violence within communities. Prison doesn't build the skills people need to be accountable for the harm they have caused. Nor does it provide a safe place to heal and unpick the cycle of violence they're caught in; indeed, many people who are abusive have experienced abuse themselves. By locking people up and subjecting them to cruelty and neglect, prison does not put anyone in a position to make better choices.

The state's label of 'violent offender' does not necessarily correlate with the harm a person has caused. Prime Minister Boris Johnson, under whose leadership more than 100,000 people have died from Covid-19 in the UK—the highest number of coronavirus deaths in Europe after Russia—is not considered violent or a risk to the public. The majority of people who died, of course, were elderly, disabled, and migrant and working-class precarious workers, while Boris Johnson is one of the most powerful people in the country. Meanwhile, some sentences mean a person who has been released from prison and then uses drugs once, misses their curfew by minutes or has a mental health crisis must immediately be recalled to prison, apparently for the protection of the public.

There is no link between the rates of crime in England and Wales and the prison population. Yet crime reduction is given as a constant justification for hiring more police officers and building new prisons. Prisons aren't eliminating crime—they're disappearing vulnerable people. The very people who are forced to rely on the state for housing, benefits and care are typically also those stuck in the cycle between prison, probation services and mental health institutions. All the while, people with access to resources and power avoid interacting with those systems entirely. This stark disparity is exacerbated as the British government makes cuts to legal aid—or assistance toward the costs of legal counsel and representation—which is increasingly difficult to access at trial and already almost impossible for adjudications taking place inside prisons.

Prisons don't do what we are told they do. It's vital to understand the mechanisms the state uses in its targeted oppression to send specific groups to prison and keep them there. While the state claims prisons 'rehabilitate', people who serve less than a year in custody are more likely to end up back in prison than not. At the same time, the state is sending more people to prison than ever, with two and a half times as many people sentenced to over ten years in 2018 as in 2006.

Life inside

Inside prisons, people are subjected to brutal and dehumanising conditions. There have been 1,785 deaths in custody in England and Wales since 1990. Conditions in the prison system in England, Wales and Scotland are among the deadliest in Europe—abuse, stigmatisation, medical neglect and isolation result in the death of a person in prison at least once every four days, according to the Ministry of Justice. Some people in prison are denied showers for six days, and Muslim people inside have been denied ritual cleansing before prayer. During the Covid-19 pandemic, it was imprisoned people who were providing full-time, comprehensive care to other people inside with chronic conditions. This is a clear contradiction with what many incarcerated people are told when they're released from prison—that they are not to be trusted with any care responsibilities and not skilled enough for most jobs.

Racism in the legal system is one of the law's fundamental functions, not an exception. Our friend Kushal Sood, a solicitor and advocate, shares that there is a lack of structural critique within the legal system. 'I think the vast majority of my peers see racist and hateful decision-making as an aberration, rather than an inevitability. Centuries of evidence isn't enough for them. The truth is that there are some people who have been prevented by this system from flourishing, or even surviving.'

A friend incarcerated in a women's prison in England shared with us that Black women are separated from each other inside, limited to two or three per wing, to stop them from 'forming gangs'. The prison uses the same racist justification to deny her access to music, while white people inside are allowed to listen to the same music. Everything costs money in prison—at extortionate prices when we consider that the minimum wage for incarcerated people is £4 a week. Black women have fought to get additional products for haircare on the list of items available to them inside, but many still struggle to pay the high price for them. One friend reported that she was ridiculed by guards for being upset when she was denied access to basic haircare products.

Imprisoned people who participate in resistance to poor treatment are put in segregation in dire conditions and are cut off from researching and contacting lawyers. Lawyers in turn aren't able to reach out without being requested to by their client, keeping people isolated from legal recourse and unable to speak out publicly regarding their treatment inside.

Under the IPP sentence ('Imprisonment for Public Protection'), criminalised people have no maximum limit on how long they can spend in prison. After their minimum term, or tariff, is served, there are many barriers preventing release—for instance, someone may be required to complete several 'rehabilitative' courses that the prison doesn't offer or denies them access to. If they are released, they are given licence conditions that result in a recall to prison for an indefinite amount of time because of any minor infraction; this can even include a mental health crisis. Although this sentence was abolished in 2012 for being inhumane, the abolishment was not applied retroactively, and on 31 December 2020, 1,849 IPP prisoners were still in prison, 95% of whom had served their minimum tariff.

Targeted criminalisation

The Crown Prosecution Service (CPS) has increasingly been targeting teenage boys, many of them people of colour, using an archaic common law doctrine known as 'joint enterprise', which means that someone can be prosecuted for a crime even if they are only distantly connected to the incident. Stop and search laws are used to target young men, boys and gender-non-conforming people of colour eight times more than white people across the same age groups. This has long been a part of everyday life for young people of colour, particularly in cities. Some of the young people we have worked with in South London recalled being stopped and having their pockets and bags searched up to three times in one day on their way home from school. Property laws and trespass laws are also used to disproportionately police and imprison Gypsy, Roma and Traveller (GRT) communities, who make up only 0.1% of the general population but 6% of those incarcerated in women's prisons.

The government's anti-terrorism PREVENT strategy has injected high levels of surveillance and policing into Muslim and South Asian lives. Its association of terrorism with Islam has provided a pretext to turn doctors, teachers and social workers into spies for the state. In 2020, Muslims made up 16% of the prison population in England and Wales, yet only 4% of the general population. While only 1% of Muslims in prison are inside for terrorism-related offences, Muslims account for half of the population of close supervision centres, the most torturous and highest-security prisons in the UK. Regardless of what they've been convicted for, Muslims are treated as if they pose a higher risk to the public and other people inside.

In response to the riots triggered by Mark Duggan's murder by police in 2011, the London Metropolitan Police, in collaboration with partnering organisations such as housing associations and job centres, created the Gangs Matrix, a racist database that lists primarily young Black men in order to target them for criminalisation. Black people are more likely to be stopped and searched, less likely to get a community sentence, more likely to be sent to prison, and more likely to get a longer sentence and worse probation conditions than white people in the same circumstances. Like many marginalised groups who already have a painful relationship with the police and the state by the time they come into contact with the courts, Black people are less likely to take a plea deal when offered, not believing the outcome will be better for them than if they plead not guilty. They are also more likely to be deemed a high enough 'risk' to need to be kept in custody. Once inside, marginalised people are kept there for longer by parole boards and probation services.

Police themselves are perpetrators of violence, but they are protected by each other and by the justice system from criminalisation. In 2021, Channel 4 News reported that in the last two years, one woman a week had come forward with accusations of domestic abuse by a partner in the police. The conviction rate of police officers accused of domestic abuse was only 3.9%—more than a third less than that of the general public. In March 2021, thirty-three-year-old Sarah Everard was abducted, raped and murdered by PC Wayne Couzens, who used his powers of arrest to handcuff and kidnap her as she was walking home in South London. Despite Couzens' conviction for these egregious acts of harm, the police continue to hold the very same coercive powers. The response of the Metropolitan Police has been to step up its presence and put even more officers on the streets—a vain attempt to claw back the narrative that police have an interest in keeping people safe from gender-based violence.

There is a deep and dark legacy of undercover policing in the UK that shows how dedicated the state is to quashing dissent. The infiltration by a police officer of the Stephen Lawrence campaign—organised by family members seeking justice for the racist murder of a Black teenager in 1993 and the racism of the police in response—is just one example illustrating the commitment of criminal justice institutions to protecting themselves from accountability and maintaining public control. Since 1968, the police have infiltrated more than a thousand activist groups, with spycops starting relationships under false identities and going as far as to father children with their targets, before abruptly returning to their real lives and families, leaving a trail of trauma and confusion in their wake. The Police Spies Out of Lives campaign uncovered the lengths to which police will go in order to undermine and disrupt relationships between people who get together to organise or support each other.

The growth of the prison industrial complex

The government is pursuing the development of bigger, rural prisons for the men's prison estate in the UK; meanwhile, the expansion of the women's estate has already led to more people incarcerated. As well as finding ways to integrate carceral punishment into communities, the state claims that prisons for young people can be educational and has also proposed specialised prisons for migrants and other marginalised groups. Prison overcrowding is a huge issue and is causing a decline in already disgusting conditions inside, especially during the Covid-19 pandemic, throughout which people have been unable to socially distance or keep themselves clean. In its plans for expansion, however, the state isn't concerned about the impact of overcrowding on people in prison. In the time being taken to build all of these prisons, the government could have released a lot of people. Far more resources are used in expanding and securitising prisons than it would take to facilitate people's wellbeing and safety without criminalising and dehumanising them.

The UK's prison population is the third largest in Europe, after Russia and Turkey, with over 90,000 people held in British prisons in early 2021, and more if we account for those in immigration and mental health detention institutions. In 2014, the government announced plans to build the first in a new line of prisons in North Wales, now the monstrosity of HMP Berwyn. The next year, Justice Secretary Michael Gove revealed plans for the construction of nine 'mega-prisons' to hold 10,000 prisoners in a massive expansion of the prison system across England, Wales and Scotland. Soon after, it was announced that HMP Holloway would be closed, and that the people imprisoned there would be moved to prisons outside of London, likely to be further from their communities and held in already overcrowded conditions. At the time of writing, this Prison Estate Transformation Programme has been superseded by the 2020 New Prisons Programme; at least 18,000 prison places are scheduled for creation across the country, and prisons have almost completely been rebuilt on old sites in Wellingborough and Glen Parva in the Midlands, meaning Gove's plan has been expanded under a new name.

There are currently plans for new types of prisons for people the state considers women; in 2021, 500 more places were scheduled for creation across the existing women's prison estate in England and new, smaller 'community units' in Scotland and Wales. The government is also creating a new model for imprisoning children between the ages of twelve and seventeen under the despicable name of 'secure schools'. In the planned expansion of Heathrow Airport, we have seen the proposal of a 'mega detention centre' to replace existing immigration detention centres—prisons specifically for people considered 'foreign nationals'.

These announcements are often used to appease public concern over horrifyingly unhygienic and overcrowded conditions and are promoted by prison officers to people inside under the guise of improvement. However, the Ministry of Justice and the Home Office are clear in their agenda: to put more police on the street and more people in prison. The government is legislating to increase criminalisation and is investing in more technology for surveillance and control within communities, such as ankle tags and facial recognition cameras. We have seen through relentless media coverage of knife crime and street violence how a thorough narrative is being coordinated to justify the more widespread usage of these technologies, paid for by the public.

One company that manufactures such technologies, like ankle tags, is G4S. In 2019, the company won a five-year multi-million-pound contract from the Scottish government to increase capacity for community policing and enforce curfews for criminalised people. G4S runs four prisons in the UK and was awarded a £300 million contract in October 2020 to run one of the new mega-prisons in Wellingborough, despite the fact that its contract to run HMP Birmingham was ended seven years early by the government as a result of the prison's horrific conditions. As reported by the European Coordination of Committees and Associations for Palestine, G4S also provides services to Israeli police forces, and thus it is one of the biggest beneficiaries and drivers of colonial policing today. Other private companies that run prisons, build prisons, or provide services to prisons and detention centres include Sodexo, Serco and Kier Group; many of these same companies are also contracted by other public institutions, such as hospitals, public transport services and universities.

In 2021, the Home Office proposed the Police, Crime, Sentencing and Courts Bill, a piece of legislation outlining an almost all-encompassing approach to policing that targets every community already marginalised by the law—sex workers, GRT communities, Black and brown people, people in prison, and young people who have been excluded and criminalised. The bill anticipates growing capacity for imprisonment through the construction of mega-prisons via the New Prisons Programme. It proposes longer sentences, and that more power be given to parole boards to make decisions preventing the release of people who are deemed too high a risk to 'public protection'. For Black people and people of colour in an already racist criminal justice system, this bill will no doubt create more barriers to regaining freedom. Black women are 25% more likely to receive a custodial sentence than white women for the same offence—we can see who will be filling up the new prison places if we allow this bill to be introduced and the New Prisons Programme to be completed.

What about prison reform?

As history has proven, prison reform enables the growth of the carceral state. After decades of reform, the prison system continues to disproportionately target poor Black and brown communities, people with disabilities and learning difficulties, and queer and trans people. Reform responds with a focus on correcting the supposed biases of individual officers, instead of recognising a structure explicitly designed to control and disempower marginalised groups. Reform means an increase in police use of body-worn cameras, which are more frequently used against people being arrested than for police accountability. Reform encourages investment in new policing technologies—and new contracts to private security companies to develop such tools. Reform means more of us put on tag, more cameras watching us everywhere we go, more laws to be used against us. More inquiries that drag on for years and lead nowhere. More people killed by bureaucracy. Our society is no safer because of bigger or better prisons, or more police, or more criminal laws; in reality, the bigger the carceral state becomes, the more violence in our societies.

Reforms have led to the New Prisons Programme and talk of 'green prisons'. To forced labour inside for a tenner a week while formerly incarcerated people still end up homeless and unemployable upon release. Reforms have led to mother-and-baby units that allow for babies to be born into prison instead of to free parents, and to art students at Central Saint Martins gaining degrees from designing ergonomic furniture for cramped prison spaces.

Reforms in the prison system always have a flipside that enables punishment and coercion. When new facilities are made available, prisons can refuse you access to those facilities. You want access to education, even university degrees, in prison? Only if you jump through certain hoops. Anything good that comes out of reform can be taken away or used to coerce someone into submission.

A friend of ours imprisoned in the North in a women's prison—a nice, reformed prison—was given a pet budgie as a perk and a test of responsibility. But when the budgie was ill, there was no way to access veterinary care. Forcing someone to sit in a cell and watch their pet suffer is a special kind of torture, only enabled by persistent campaigns to improve conditions inside prisons in superficial ways, which could never make a material difference within an institution whose very purpose is dehumanisation.

2.

BRICK BY BRICK: THE DISMANTLING

In breaking down the systems that need to be dismantled, we want to show how the carceral state is embedded in every aspect of our lives. We didn't have the space to cover everything! Alongside friends and activists, we've tried to begin the work of uncovering the bricks of the prison industrial complex that structure our world. Each of these short sections could be a book in itself, or a lengthy workshop series. We hope they inspire you to do your own learning and exploration.

In the following sections, we undertake an honest and critical look at the reality of many of the systems that shape British society. Content may be disturbing or upsetting, so please look after yourself as you're reading.

1.

IMPERIALISM

Every society inherits a legacy from the past. To understand any institution or power structure, we need to look at its history. In what context were systems of state violence created, and what purpose were they serving? Most of modern British history is a history of empire; for centuries before colonised peoples fought for and won their independence, Britain was an empire.

As Britain expanded its empire, new forms of control and violence were required to subjugate colonised and enslaved populations. Through examining the state's long history of using prisons, policing and other forms of punishment as tools of imperial domination, we find that Britain's criminal justice system as we know it today first emerged as a product of slavery, imperialism and colonialism.

Imperialism is the exercise of state power to influence or dominate for the purpose of expanding the sphere of the state's economic and political control. This can manifest in direct, obvious ways (military occupation, settler colonialism), or it can take more subtle forms (economic imperialism). Colonialism and colonisation often make up a key part of imperialism. They refer to the practice of territorial expansion through seizure of land and domination over colonised people, for the purpose of bringing economic and political benefit to the colonising country.

As an imperial power, Britain enslaved and subjugated millions across the world; today it continues to organise arms and security fairs that sell weaponry and surveillance equipment to target their descendants. Imperialism is inherently exploitative and extractive, and it requires violence to sustain its control. While imperial nations may claim to invade under the pretext of 'civilising' people and protecting them from violence, we know they wield the same physical and sexual violence as their tools of domination. It was through this project that a global system of imprisonment and policing was developed. During the Enlightenment, prisons were even imagined to be an example of the triumph of humanist liberal ideals and universal human rights, even though these supposedly universal ideals ignored non-European, Indigenous, racialised and colonised people. Race and racial hierarchy were constructed and enshrined in law to justify the violence necessary for imperial rule.

The legacy of imperial and state violence and punishment is still present today in the very infrastructure of former colonies. Jamaica and Nigeria still have active prisons constructed by the British during the colonial period, such as the Kirikiri Maximum Security Prison, built in Nigeria in 1955. The first prisons in the West Indies, many of which are still standing, were built by the British. Policing, too, became a standard of so-called 'civilisation'. We notice this legacy within the history of the Royal Barbados Police Force, first established in 1835 under British rule and modelled after the London Metropolitan Police until today.

We cannot talk about abolition without talking about slavery—and the movement to abolish it. Britain often credits itself for its role in the abolition of the slave trade, but who started it, and who was profiteering from it? And who decided to compensate not those enslaved but the slavers for their 'loss of property' once slavery was abolished?

The British criminal justice system, so often vaunted by civil servants as 'the envy of the world', provided the legal framework to sustain slavery. Slavery was defined in and reinforced by law, which gave slavers the power to use violence to control people. Tools and tactics for suppressing anti-slavery rebellions in Guyana and Jamaica were developed and justified by the need to retain imperial power and enforce labour—this was the birth of the prison and military industrial complex.

Even after rebellions by enslaved people against their oppressors brought about the abolition of slavery, the state adopted still more coercive forms of policing, prisons and punishment. New laws were enforced to criminalise people who had been enslaved or descendants of enslaved people, codifying their class status. In Guyana, a British colonial law criminalising gender non-conformity, which was used to target many queer people and sex workers, was not repealed until 2018. Vagrancy laws, sex work criminalisation and anti-trespass laws were all used to reinforce the colonial status quo.

These methods of suppression and increasingly militarised policing, developed for the purpose of colonial control in one place, would travel, exported from one colony to another, until eventually the same tools were used to quash dissent in the imperial metropole. Tear gas was frequently used in the 1930s by the British in India and the Caribbean, and these tools were not used closer to the British mainland until 1969 to suppress the Irish in Northern Ireland. Tear gas and violent armed police tactics were then unleashed on anti-racist/Black uprisings in the 1980s in Great Britain itself, in Liverpool.

Prisons were first seen as a more humane method of punishment than state-mandated execution or mutilation. Working-class British subjects, who were criminalised through laws similar to those we have today, were either executed or transported en masse to populate the penal colonies in New South Wales, Australia, from 1778. In this way, through colonialism, the logic of punishment and criminal justice spread, taking hold and lasting to this day.

Even after slavery abolition and decolonisation, imperial states continue to control and dominate people of the Global South today in order to maintain extractive capitalism.

In 2011, Britain tried to 'gift' a prison to Jamaica to which they would deport migrants from the UK. The Jamaican government rejected this proposal. In 2019, a plan to build a British prison in Nigeria was also rejected by the Nigerian government. These attempts to perpetuate the incarceration of people in the former colonies is what we call carceral colonialism.

Empire birthed the military industrial complex, an entire industry of private war-profiteering companies created and enriched by imperial violence. This industry wants to sustain itself and grow, driven by the capitalist imperative to accrue wealth through exploitation and expropriation. Many of the same private security companies that run violent prisons in Britain also manufacture equipment used by the military. Violence is, after all, profitable.

Military violence has long been a tool of empire, and neo-imperial states continue to profit from the very same violence today. In 1917, the British government issued the Balfour Declaration, which announced support for the establishment of a Jewish state in Palestine and paved the way for the creation of Israel as a settler colony. In 1936–1939, when Palestinian people rebelled against the British Mandate in the Great Revolt, the British Army responded with severe military repression, killing thousands. Britain's role in the oppression of Palestinians doesn't start with its continued sale of arms to Israel today—the British enabled the expulsion of Palestinians from their homes in the first place.

In 2010–2019, despite resistance from the public, the UK followed the USA as the second biggest arms exporter in the world, selling £86 billion worth of arms. This included sales to twenty-two of the thirty countries on the government's own human rights watch list, such as Saudi Arabia, which is waging a brutal war against Yemen in which homes, hospitals and schools have been bombed. The British government claims to condemn these human rights violations, yet it participates in that very violence by selling military weapons and equipment to regimes responsible for war crimes and repression around the world. This is the face of modern imperialism, as Britain's incessant enrichment continues to wreak death and destruction in the Global South.

2.

CRIMMIGRATION

In a process of neoliberal globalisation, borders, immigration legislation and bureaucracy prevent the mobility of human beings while international trade agreements permit capital to move freely around the world. For British corporations, labour is more easily exploitable in the Global South, where wages are lower, and so industry is increasingly outsourced for the sake of profit. As a result, the UK's de-industrialised communities have suffered huge levels of unemployment, while the state has continually cut social services through decades of austerity. Not only do mass job losses and the destruction of communities turn people into perfect candidates for prison, as Angela Davis argues in *Are Prisons Obsolete?*, but increased policing and criminalisation of the state's citizens are also coupled with immigration law enforcement, detention and deportation. In this way, the state evades responsibility for social problems by scapegoating and punishing minoritised individuals.

Globalisation, capitalism and imperialism together have created a system of 'crimmigration'—the combination of criminal law and immigration law—aimed at controlling the poor, disposing of undesirables and maintaining the nation state's power. These interlocking social, economic and political systems have resulted in both mass incarceration in the Global North and the mass exodus of war refugees from the

Global South. National border control benefits businesses and employers by dividing workers, forcing unemployment and fostering despair. Both Labour and Tory governments have long been hell-bent on controlling the borders, and Home Secretary Priti Patel is only the newest face in an old story.

The issues faced by migrants range from homelessness and poverty to imprisonment and deportation, all of which are actively perpetuated by the British government. In 2012, then Home Secretary Theresa May introduced a set of 'hostile environment' policies, which converted everyone working in the public sector into immigration agents. The lives of undocumented migrants became extremely difficult, as police, NHS workers, employers, landlords and universities were all advised to check immigration status. This caused a rise in fear among migrants of using necessary public services, due to the risk of being reported and detained.

In order to dismantle xenophobic Brexit Britain, we must first break down the relationship between the border and the law. When applied to immigration, logics that justify incarceration in prisons are extended to other aspects of our lives, including education, social services and public health. Undocumented migrants in the UK are policed and punished by the Border Force and immigration detention and are given second-class status through exclusion from housing and social support. Border control functions are passed on to private entities such as airlines and security companies, or to local and civil officials such as police officers and airport employees. The border invades our communities by making everyone around us accountable to the Home Office. Migrants become the enemy, and those who fail to report them are also deemed criminals. All of this is justified by the state in the name of security and 'the national interest'.

The truth is that citizenship takes precedence over humanity and dignity in our society. Members of Cradle have been pushed out of work, experienced risk of homelessness and suffered food poverty as a result of our migration status. 'No Recourse to Public Funds' conditions exclude some migrants from access to benefits, with the goal of driving us into poverty and eventually making us leave the country. In reality, these laws push migrant workers into informal, labour-intensive and highly exploitative work just to stay afloat. Through the denial of basic human needs, such as access to financial support for food and housing, immigration legislation punishes people for not having citizenship and residency documents.

The government and media put a lot of money and effort into making sure the mistreatment of migrants is perceived as a distant problem in the UK. As a member state of the European Union, the UK pushed the issue of border securitisation out to the Mediterranean Sea—far enough away that the violence of border control could be kept hidden from the general public in Britain. It was not until 2015, at the height of the sensationalised European migrant crisis, that international news broadcasted shocking visuals that demonstrated the human cost of British and European border policy. But the story mostly wasn't reported this way—instead of focusing on the violence of border control, blame and responsibility were shifted onto people smugglers, or even migrants themselves. In reality, policies in place with the deliberate aim of making crossing borders difficult, in an attempt to deter migration, put people in serious danger and raise the number of migrant deaths. The EU and the UK even choose to ignore migrant boats and prevent rescue missions so as not to 'encourage' further migration.

Language itself can present an obstacle in discussions about migrant justice. The government, media and policy makers use a variety of terms, ranging from 'immigrants' to 'asylum seekers'. Each term has evolved over time to hold a subtle set of associations. The word 'illegal' is added to 'immigrants' to connote criminality and has driven the narrative that certain migrants are more deserving than others. Labels like 'economic migrants' and 'voluntary migrants' are used in propaganda to describe people who move for a better quality of life, often with the implication that their motivations for migration are selfish and illegitimate. By contrast, refugees and asylum seekers, who have been forcibly displaced by conflict or fear of persecution, are routinely dehumanised and presented as a drain on the state's economic resources. The crisis narrative in the media has encouraged public hostility towards perceived large numbers of migrants, when in reality only about 0.3% of the UK's population are refugees and asylum seekers.

In August 2020, UK media was flooded with images of camps in Calais and boats filled with migrants making the journey across the English Channel. The Home Office responded by shifting blame onto France and 'criminal gangs', requesting military personnel and converting army barracks into housing for migrants. While the government maintains that the army barracks are not detention centres, the rapidly increasing rate of Covid infections and lack of safe and sanitary living conditions have drawn criticism from many charities and grassroots organisations.

The humanity of migrants often isn't acknowledged until it's too late. This was made clear in October 2019, when thirty-nine Vietnamese people were found dead in a refrigerated trailer in Essex and subsequently mourned by the same state that made it impossible for them to migrate in safety. Frontex, Europe's border patrol agency, justifies disrupting migrant treks across the Mediterranean as 'protecting human life'. While it's true that hundreds of people drown annually on makeshift boats in the Mediterranean and the Channel, this framing leaves out the direct role of the state in endangering human life through its persecution and criminalisation of migrants.

In Britain, coercive methods of immigration control are justified by the Home Office as 'risk reduction' and deterrence. The distinction between immigration law and criminal justice enforcement is repeatedly blurred, from the oversight of immigration removal centres (IRCs) by Her Majesty's Prison Service

(HMPS), to the existence of multiple 'foreign national offender' prisons, intended to streamline deportations at the end of custodial sentences. In this system, even the pretence of being proportional has gone out the window. Xenophobia easily crosses between administrative and criminal law, using whichever is easier to target and remove undocumented people. Research by Sarah Turnbull and Ines Hasselberg shows that many migrants imprisoned in HMP Huntercombe, a prison in Oxfordshire, no longer expected to be released back into their community in Britain upon the end of their sentences; instead, they believed they would inevitably either remain in prison as immigration detainees or be transferred to an IRC.

Legislation for holding 'unwanted' migrants in custody emerged in the UK in the mid-1980s as neoliberalism took hold. In fact, the privatisation of detention centres predates that of other prisons, and today the same multinational conglomerates that run private prisons also run IRCs. The UK continues to favour the use of migrant detention, with seven IRCs across the country and 23,970 immigration detainees in 2020, including children, according to the Global Detention Project. While the government does not categorise them as such, IRCs are a type of prison, though people inside are permitted a few more basic rights than others within state prisons, such as the right to have personal phones. For years, reports and experiences have been shared on ongoing issues inside IRCs, including physical violence, sexual assault, deaths in custody, deterioration of mental health, lack of adequate healthcare, unsanitary living conditions and the separation of families. The reality of IRCs mirrors that of prisons—a sign that both require more than reform.

The supposed purpose of IRCs, as per the Detention Centre Rules 2001, is to provide 'secure but humane accommodation', with the end goal of forcibly removing people, often sending them to countries with which they have little to no connection, or where they even face severe threat. Most people convicted in the criminal justice system are given a definite sentence, although some are not. Immigration detention, however, is indefinite, and the threat of sudden deportation hangs over those imprisoned in these centres, causing huge amounts of stress.

The growing legislative overlap between criminal and immigration offenses, the violent policing of the border, and the similarities in the experiences of those within prisons and immigration detention centres demonstrate clearly the British state's enforcement of carceral practices with regard to migration. Despite the UK's formal ratification of international human rights treaties, its treatment of migrants has remained inhumane.

3.

ENVIRONMENTAL PUNISHMENT

As each summer becomes hotter in the UK, the lack of air conditioning in prisons becomes more and more dangerous. Across the world, we clearly see the deadly consequences of prioritising punishment over health every time that natural disasters, such as hurricanes, hit prisons that still don't have plans in place for evacuating the people inside. Even outside prisons, environmental punishment primarily impacts people in the Global South and poor and racialised communities in the Global North, who suffer destruction of their land and homes and bear the brunt of flooding, droughts and severe health consequences from air pollution.

Britain was built upon the extraction of nature's resources at devastating levels. 'The continued culture of extraction is the major force that guides us into the climate crisis. That same root is shared with police and prisons,' explains Orion, a climate justice and youth organiser in the so-called USA. In fact, Western governments and private corporations even employ military and policing tactics abroad in order to extract the natural resources needed to maintain the lifestyle they desire. Wars are fought to control fossil fuels, and communities are displaced and poisoned in order to build oil and fracking pipelines. Those impacted are violently criminalised and even killed for their resistance.

Our friend Mama Julz is an Oglala Lakota grandmother who grew up on the Pine Ridge Reservation and works on the front-line of the resistance to pipeline construction across Turtle Island (also known as North America). She was the first person to chain herself to excavating equipment at the Dakota Access Pipeline in Standing Rock. She fights tirelessly to protect sacred lands, water and Indigenous communities from the inevitable destruction caused by pipeline construction. She has been violently arrested by the police at least six times for taking direct action. Her experience and that of hundreds of others teach us of the true brutality that confronts us when we go head-to-head with these extractive forces.

At the same time, in California, incarcerated people are forced to fight wildfires, which themselves are an ecologically disastrous result of a long history of mismanagement of the land since the colonisers' arrival. Criminalised people are exploited and made to work in severely dangerous situations to literally fight the fires resulting from capitalist exploitation. For those who are released from prison, this life-threatening experience rarely means it's easier to get a job, even as a firefighter.

The ecological devastation caused by the British empire evolved alongside racial control. As a result of the changing climate, countries in the Caribbean such as Jamaica and Guyana, where the British were responsible for building early prisons, have experienced severe changes in rainfall, leading to flooding and agricultural destruction. In the UK, 83% of the London primary schools that are exposed to illegal levels of air pollution are in working-class communities. People of colour in the UK are 50% more likely to live in an area with poor air quality than their white counterparts. Wherever we end up, we bear the brunt of the climate crisis. This amounts to targeted environmental violence.

When considering the environment through the lens of abolition, we must also account for the impact of prisons and policing on our health and on the land. Thousands of people are trapped in prisons and detention centres designed to punish via poor-quality air, water and food, alongside restricted access to personal hygiene and basic healthcare. These toxic conditions have been made even more deadly by the rapid spread of Covid-19 in the prison system.

Her Majesty's Prison Service has no hesitation in choosing to build its cages in rural areas on contaminated land, such as on sites formerly used to store nuclear energy. Prison construction companies have a track record of rejecting sustainable materials to meet requirements for securitisation by the Ministry of Justice. New prisons pledge to reach the 'excellent' score on their environmental assessments, but this is nothing more than a tick-box exercise. Proper ventilation and heating, for example, do not necessarily apply across every cell.

In response to environmental concerns regarding prisons, 'sustainable prisons' are put forward as a solution. In this way, the state uses ideas of 'innovation' in so-called green tech and design to justify the construction of new prisons. The corporations responsible for bringing these innovations into the expansion of the prison and policing systems are rarely questioned in the mainstream or by environmentalists.

Reformists have long called for prisons to be made more 'environmentally friendly', without recognising that prisons are themselves a symptom of capitalism's destructive relationship with the land. Prisons, even new ones, quickly become overcrowded and create immense damage to the surrounding environment. Beyond issues of the land itself, the toxicity of prisons runs all the way through the experience for those imprisoned there. Drinking dirty water, eating poor-quality, contaminated food, breathing polluted air, being denied sunlight and community, and being subjected to regular abuse are all experiences that are deeply poisonous to our bodies and our minds. Experiencing them all at once for long, long periods of time shortens lives.

4.

FOOD POVERTY

People trapped in food poverty either struggle to afford nutritious food or live in a 'food desert' without access to fresh food they can buy cheaply. An estimated 8 million people in Britain are experiencing the violence of food poverty, with the worst hit being people of colour and disabled and older people.

Fifty-five per cent of Britain's food is sourced domestically, with the rest imported from other countries, mostly from the EU. Though the proportion of food we import from the Global South is small—4% from African countries, for instance—many communities across Africa and Latin America remain hugely dependent on Britain for the sale of sugar, cocoa, tea and spices. They provide a large proportion of goods considered fundamental to British culture; for example, over 40% of the tea we drink is grown in Kenya. The food we eat is historically and directly tied to legacies of colonialism and the rise of racial capitalism. The production and trade of sugar, cocoa for chocolate, and tea and spices have been used to justify enslavement, genocide, community displacement and environmental destruction across Africa, Asia and the Caribbean.

People farming in the Global South are often restricted by neo-colonial trade agreements. Some are sanctioned for growing food for their own communities if their land is owned for the purpose of production and export, as is the case for many farmers in countries such as Zimbabwe and Barbados. Food grown locally is expensive for people living in these regions, but the same food is sold cheaply in the UK.

Back in Britain, under Tory rule, we've seen a huge increase in the number of working people plunged into food poverty. According to the Child Poverty Action Group, around 72% of kids in families struggling to afford food have at least one parent who works. Decades of cuts to public services led 2.5 million to need to rely on food bank charities in the year 2020–21. Welfare 'reforms', such as the introduction of Universal Credit, which leaves many people waiting for five weeks before being given any money, penalise those in insecure work. In 2020, as Covid lockdown restrictions slashed our incomes, the British government spent around £850 million on the 'Eat Out to Help Out' scheme, rather than directly redistributing money to those who needed it.

The government applies punishment to food poverty in the form of benefit sanctions, when welfare payments are stopped or reduced as a penalty for failure to fulfil the state's requirements, like attending appointments and interviews. People can be sanctioned for things like missing a meeting with their 'work coach' at the local job centre because they were looking after their sick child. Additionally, the Department for Work and Pensions (DWP) often simply makes mistakes and cancels payments for no reason. The re-drawing of benefits for disabled people has meanwhile led to hundreds of cases where people have been dragged into food poverty as they are suddenly deemed 'fit for work' and stop receiving benefits.

A friend imprisoned in a women's prison in the South East of England reported to us that the food in prison is of poor quality, badly prepared and lacking in nutrition, often being carb-heavy. When she was put in an isolation room after testing positive for Covid-19, the food that was delivered to her door was a piece of meat that looked 'green and scaly'. The prison administration often refuses to meet people's dietary requirements, such as eating halal, being vegetarian or eating gluten-free. In the same prison, a Muslim who eats halal was lied to by the officers, who turned out not to know what halal meant.

Even in state prisons, food for people inside is supplied through contracts with private companies, who are motivated only by profit and not by providing good-quality food. These companies are paid vast amounts to provide 'catering' and 'facilities management', but we know that people serving prison sentences actually do most of the work of maintaining prisons, including food prep and cleaning.

Inside and outside prison, the criminalisation of fatness can have huge consequences for families. In March 2021, *The Guardian* reported that two teens in West Sussex had been separated from their working-class parents and put into care, despite what the judge described as a case of 'a loving family' with 'some very good parenting'. The reason? Fatphobia. The parents were deemed neglectful because their children had been labelled obese.

Fatness is associated with being working-class, and it is therefore criminalised in a way that being 'underweight' isn't. The idea that this is out of concern for the wellbeing of obese children is clearly false—middle-class kids who are deemed underweight aren't being separated from their parents, despite the fact that more people die from anorexia than from any other eating disorder.

Our ideas about good and bad bodies and about which people are deserving of healthcare, resources and life are rooted in colonial ideas about savage Black bodies. In the 1810s, Sarah Baartman, a South African Khoikhoi woman, was sold and exhibited naked in cages in Europe because she was fat and Black. Cesare Lombroso, a nineteenth-century Italian scientist, credited with coining the term 'criminology', believed that sex workers' criminality was linked to fatness and Blackness, markers of primitiveness. More recently, in 2019, the lawyers representing Daniel Pantaleo, the officer who murdered Eric

Garner in New York City in 2014, stated in court that Garner did not die as a result of police violence but rather 'from being morbidly obese'. Fatphobia is inextricable from the anti-Blackness that sustains the carceral state.

Today, the NHS uses the BMI (Body Mass Index) calculator to determine which bodies are worth treating and places adverts warning about an obesity epidemic. These metrics perpetuate the idea that fat people are the problem in society and that we should fear fatness, using a logic similar to that which the state has historically leveraged against Black people. There is no ideal weight, ideal size or ideal body type—our bodies are varied and neutral. Our ideas around particular bodies being good or bad are rooted in the same binaries that the state uses to police and control our lives.

Ultimately, our demands when it comes to food poverty are too low. The 'free school meals' battle led by footballer Marcus Rashford was hard won in November 2020, when the British government finally agreed to feed children living in poverty over the school holidays. But money was dutifully doled out to private catering companies, rather than to families directly to buy their groceries. These 'hampers' that were supposed to cover £30 worth of food for ten days contained a measly loaf of bread, some cheese, a tin of beans, two carrots, two bananas, three apples, two potatoes, a plastic bag of pasta, three Frubes yoghurts, two Soreen loaf bars and a tomato. We deserve so, so much more. We deserve to have access to safe, nourishing food and the joy of having time to gather with loved ones for a meal.

5.

HEALTHCARE IN HANDCUFFS

During perhaps the biggest ongoing global health crisis in modern history—the Covid-19 pandemic—all people in prison should have been released from their cages to seek safety, socially distance, exercise outdoors and access healthy food, just like anyone else. Instead, despite recommendations from public health authorities and even prison governors themselves, people inside were left completely exposed to the rapid spread of Covid throughout the prison system. What kind of society do we live in where the label of 'criminal' takes priority over the label of 'human' when it comes to our right to health?

Whether the state kills us directly or not, many layers of oppression cut some lives short, while the powerful live long, healthy lives at others' expense. Our healthcare system mirrors the criminal justice system, reacting to sickness as opposed to preventing it, and then compelling us to report what's going on with our bodies or minds to an institution that responds professionally to illness. Bureaucratising healthcare within the state's capitalist structure has dissociated people from their basic health needs and serves to eradicate existing knowledge of medicine and care within communities. Abolition is an issue of public health.

The UK prides itself on having a universal healthcare system accessible to all and free at the point of use, but this isn't actually the case. Healthcare is denied in prisons, to those without immigration status, to those who have bodies that fall outside of the status quo, and to people who have been diagnosed with psychiatric disorders. Survival itself is criminalised when any person is arrested for stealing food or for sharing medication with others who are denied treatment. People are not believed to know what they need, especially when they are marginalised by the state.

The mainstream Western understanding of medicine is rooted in colonialism and was built by people invested in and benefiting from slavery. As Britain expanded its empire across the world, advances in medical care became another powerful tool to justify its violence across the Global South. Foundational gynaecological research has recently been exposed as having been developed through experimentation on enslaved women. The practice of exploitative medical testing on people from the Global South continued into the 1980s and beyond, with women of colour in Britain being given long-term contraceptive injections without being fully informed of their effects. The international health industry continues to control the Global South to this day through blocking access to treatment, such as patented Covid-19 vaccinations. This is another layer of punishment built into white supremacy. Advances in knowledge and healthcare technology should be made for the good of the people, not for profit.

Even as the NHS comes under attack from increasing privatisation, it is vital to recognise the experiences of oppressed people within this seemingly benign institution—no institution in a nation founded on white supremacy is beyond critique. Throughout the Covid-19 pandemic, Black and South Asian people have died at about twice the rate of white people in the UK. This is nothing new—a machine designed to maintain a healthy workforce under capitalism, the healthcare system depends on our people's labour and sacrifices their lives for the benefit of the elite. Britain has always relied on workers from formerly colonised countries to build and sustain the NHS, whilst restricting the same people's access to healthcare and treating them harmfully in hospitals.

Today, Black women in the UK are four times as likely to die during childbirth as white women. 'We're more vulnerable in pregnancy, but this highlights a system-wide issue,' says Dr Annabel Sowemimo of Decolonising Contraception. She refers to how healthcare professionals are more likely to listen to 'a white, middle-class patient who is telling us how they think this medical encounter should go' than someone who faces barriers to navigating the system, whether due to language, illiteracy or other issues. Professionals often respond to these patients by expressing 'irritation because they think it takes too long. Those are the patients we should actually be taking more care of.' A family member of our friend and Black community organiser Donald Mbeutcha died because the hospital staff allowed her to bleed out, ignoring her when she said something was wrong. There has been no avenue for the hospital to take accountability for this harm.

'Healthcare is used to justify the criminalisation of people,' says Sarah Lasoye, writer and activist with Race & Health, when we speak about how policing interacts with healthcare. If someone is criminalised and subsequently diagnosed with a mental health condition, this is considered by the state to be a positive outcome in both healthcare and criminal justice terms. However, many Black people who have a psychiatric diagnosis, particularly for racialised disorders such as schizophrenia ('Black men are always diagnosed with schizophrenia, never with depression,' Annabel observes), suffer from disproportionately high rates of diabetes, high blood pressure and other health conditions that are ignored. Due to the exclusive focus on their mental health diagnosis, vulnerable people are often blamed for other serious symptoms of sickness and told they have failed to look after themselves.

Hospitals and other healthcare institutions are under increasing surveillance, with the Home Office becoming ever more present. The government has introduced a surcharge to immigration applications that requires migrants to pay a several-hundred-pound fee to access healthcare. Nick Watts, director of Together with Migrant Children, refers to a situation in which he was supporting a young child with a life-threatening chronic illness. The child was put in serious danger, first by being delayed access to treatment through the NHS because their asylum application was still in progress, and then by being prevented from taking essential medication because the family were victims of an immigration enforcement raid. The fact that a child's life can be put at risk because they don't have the correct immigration papers, while around 1 in 7 people working for the NHS are migrants, is symptomatic of the disposability mindset that drives nationalism and racial capitalism.

Going to prison doesn't just mean losing your freedom—it also means losing access to adequate healthcare, and having all agency removed from you when it comes to your treatment. Incarcerated people have some of the poorest health in the country. Prisons do not provide any preventative healthcare, such as dental check-ups or pap smears. Most healthcare issues are managed within the prison, unless someone needs to be hospitalised—though our sources inside have reported that even then, prison officers delay or refuse this outright until something life-threatening happens. One of our friends imprisoned in the South of England told us that throughout 2020, people infected with Covid-19 were even denied paracetamol for several days after testing positive for the virus. Others are delayed from accessing urgent treatment. After Annabella Landsberg, a Black diabetic woman in her forties, died in Sodexo-run HMP Peterborough following physical restraint by officers, an inquest found that the prison's failure to provide healthcare for her chronic illness had probably contributed to her death. Natasha Chin died in another Sodexo-run prison,

HMP Bronzefield, less than thirty-six hours after she entered. None of the prison staff came to help her when she vomited continuously for nine hours prior to her death. An inquest concluded that her death was caused by the prison's failure to provide 'basic care', with medical experts telling the coroner's court that she would have likely survived had she received the right treatment.

While an NHS watchdog reported that almost half of prisons fail to provide adequate healthcare, in truth the standard conditions inside any prison are profoundly harmful to the bodies and minds of the people trapped inside its walls. Unsanitary living conditions are built into the punishment system, with: a lack of sunlight and vitamin D, no fresh air or space to exercise, and cramped cells with a toilet right next to the bed or no toilet at all, meaning some people are forced to urinate in their sinks at night. If loneliness in the general population is considered to increase our risk of heart disease, stroke and high blood pressure, isolation, daily dehumanisation and disconnection from loved ones will have the same, if not worse, impact on people in prison. This treatment is violent, and these institutions are killing us.

6.

INSECURE HOUSING

Housing is an essential condition for safety. But in our society, homeless people, who lack this safety themselves, are judged as threats to 'public safety' and punished accordingly—under the 1824 Vagrancy Act, begging and rough sleeping continue to be criminalised. Across Britain, there are currently more empty houses than homeless people, but rather than address the chronic housing crisis that makes this possible, society blames people for poverty and discourages the public from giving change to homeless people because 'they'll spend it on drugs'. Instead, donations are encouraged to homelessness charities like St Mungo's, who in 2019 were forced to apologise for reporting migrant rough sleepers to the Home Office. Meanwhile, local councils and private developers have installed anti-homeless architecture to reduce the number of places to sleep outside, as if forcing people off the streets means they will somehow find a comfortable bed instead.

Those without housing are denied the right to access public space, and as streets are increasingly policed and surveilled, people sleeping rough can risk arrest. Limited choices force people into dangerous living situations, vulnerable to violence and exploitation. The temporary shelters and hostels available to homeless people replicate the precarity of rough sleeping and are subject to police and immigration surveillance. The government has spent billions building new prison places, yet homeless people are released from prison with just a sleeping bag. As our friend Milly G. Ali shares, 'Homeless people are physically chucked around, treated as disposable, bounced from prisons to the street to overcrowded hostels. When you're not allowed to exist in specific spaces, your body is being ricocheted—it's policing in a very intimate way.'

In the UK, a stable address is needed to access healthcare, obtain a passport, find a job or be granted parole in prison. These conditions on static residence do not derive from nature but rather from capitalist notions of property and 'hard work'. Home ownership is seen as evidence of productivity, despite the fact that most working people are closer to homelessness than home ownership. The possibility of buying a house is becoming increasingly dependent on family inheritance, as housing prices have tripled over the past twenty years whilst wages have remained stagnant.

Most people today must live according to the unregulated whims of rich private landlords, who often refuse to maintain liveable conditions for their tenants. As Milly points out, 'If you are living with somebody that's not related to you, the landlord's got to apply for a specific kind of licence [House in Multiple Occupation], so nuclear families and straight people are usually favoured. What does that do to chosen families and living with a different kind of support network, a different kind of family? Bureaucracy within housing and land ownership leaves room for exclusion. There's a lot of policing going on in very subtle ways.' The fragmentation of housing provision and the instability of renting almost inevitably leads to alienation. People who don't know if they'll be neighbours in six months' time have very little incentive to get to know each other, or to get involved in wider community affairs.

Since Margaret Thatcher introduced the Right to Buy scheme in 1980, allowing tenants to purchase their council homes and shifting the government's goal from providing affordable public housing toward private property ownership, housing policy has become increasingly punitive. In 2011, entire families were forcibly evicted from social housing as a punishment for young people's crimes in the London riots. The new Police, Crime, Sentencing and Courts Bill proposes to force Gypsies, Roma and Travellers into homelessness by making trespassing a criminal offence and giving police the power to seize GRT homes. Working-class people are often refused planning permission to build permanent housing on land in the countryside and are then stigmatised by other local residents for living in caravans or other temporary housing. Marginalised communities are further denied housing through gentrification, when affluent, white people move to working-class areas with cheap rents, raising the rent prices in doing so and pricing poor and racialised people out of their homes. This was the case in the late 1990s with New Labour's urban regeneration policies, which encouraged 'positive gentrification' as a way to displace our communities. While asset ownership has been sold to our generation as a substitute safety net, the privatisation of social housing and rising housing prices have made this unattainable for the vast majority.

People in social housing are often forced to get by in shoddy, mouldy living conditions, leaving them with countless health issues. Local councils would rather make their residents live on demolition sites than provide safe housing, as in the case of Marian Court, a council estate in Hackney, London that was knocked down in March 2021 while a family was still living inside. Deregulation in housing policy means thousands of homes are allowed to become unsafe and to be left in disrepair, placing the tenants in harm's way.

Former squatter and social housing resident Rif tells us, 'You don't have choice, just like if you were on the streets. When you are offered social housing, you used to be given multiple housing offers, and now [with some local councils] you only get one [direct] offer. If you refuse that offer, you are deemed to have made yourself intentionally homeless, which then removes the council's responsibility to have to house you.' Within the public housing sector and housing charities, punishment and coercion are embedded into the support vulnerable people receive. A tenancy agreement for supported housing may come with restrictions on your activities—you may have a curfew, or be mandated to engage with a support worker, social worker or drug or alcohol services. Homelessness should never be used as a threat, yet it is routinely wielded against marginalised groups to control and discipline.

It was within the context of neoliberal ideology—of decades of privatisation, cuts to social housing, gentrification and deregulation—that the deaths of seventy-two people were made possible on 14 June 2017 in the Grenfell Tower fire in Kensington, London. That so many working-class people of colour lost their lives because dangerous flammable cladding saved money and looked nicer demonstrates the meeting of the carceral logic of 'cleaning up the streets' with oppressive capitalist housing policies. In the carceral state, death is profitable, and as of 2021, some of the Grenfell survivors have yet to be rehomed. Now, let's go count the empty mansions in that area.

7.

CARE UNDER THE SYSTEM

A disturbing UK-wide survey conducted by the National Society for the Prevention of Cruelty to Children (NSPCC) in 2011 showed that a quarter of eighteen- to twenty-four-year-olds reported experiencing abuse as a child. We all like to think of ourselves as very concerned for the safety of children, so why is child abuse so common in this country?

First, we have to think about the conditions that create child abuse. Many of us know well that when we are young, adults around us don't listen to us. An adult's word carries more weight than our own, and people can take advantage of the fact that an adult will be believed over a child. We are vulnerable to those we depend on, and a person who is hurting us may be the same person who is supposed to help us understand when something isn't okay—unfortunately, it is often the case that the person in a household who controls the money enacts the violence. We learn to fear punishment from an early age, and many of us have our boundaries violated or are never given a chance to develop them in the first place. We might not have the words to name our experience, and our families often don't have the tools needed to work through conflict or repair harm. When adults don't bother to apologise for making a mistake, children and young people learn to do the same—as well as the lesson that adults can treat people however they want. Too many of us carry deep generational trauma, replicating the harms enacted on us with our own kids.

Child abuse exists across class, race and ethnicity, but often it is poorer communities, especially migrants, people of colour and Gypsies, Roma and Travellers (GRT), who are targeted by state interventions. These interventions, resulting in separation from our loved ones, whether by police or social workers, often do further damage to our families and relationships. The state care system is not the way to end generational cycles of violence or create healing between parents and children—these are not even its intentions. Single parents are punished for not spending enough time with their children but aren't supported to access the resources for childcare or to work different hours. Young people in the care system report being stigmatised by other children at school whose parents tell them not to befriend them, and many experience abuse within foster placements and group homes. GRT children are increasingly taken into care, yet their culture is unlikely to be recognised or supported in their placement. Children whose primary language isn't English may be placed in homes where they are encouraged to speak English, which can create further cultural distance between the child and their parents. Care also disrupts a child's education and increases their chances of being excluded from school sevenfold.

Child abuse and sexual violence are rife at the centres of capitalist power, both today and historically. The history of child abuse by colonisers includes the rejection and even sale of their own mixed-race children. In Canada, over 200 unmarked graves of children from the Tk'emlúps te Secwépemc community were recently found buried near Kamloops Indian Residential School, an institution founded in 1893 that settler colonisers forced Indigenous children to attend in order to isolate them from their families and culture. This is not the first time that abuse has been revealed at one of these sites, which were only closed in the 1990s. We look at this history and can see how pointless it is to look to systems invested in upholding white supremacy to keep children safe.

In the UK, when a parent is deemed unfit to look after their child, the family court issues a care order and the child is taken into the so-called care of the local authority, becoming a 'looked-after child'. From there, about three quarters are placed in a foster home, often more than once over their time in the care system; only about 3% are adopted; and some are placed in children's homes. Many children are taken into care because their primary carer is in prison—only 9% of children whose primary carer is taken to a women's prison are looked after by their other parent. A 2018 report by the University of Bedfordshire found parents with disabilities were often seen as risks to their children, requiring surveillance by social services instead of additional support. Black people are disproportionately represented in the care system and experience the longest delays in placement and adoption. There are extremely high levels of child abuse in the care system, and many children go missing. Under the state's care, young people are watched and controlled, yet they are still exposed to abuse.

The interaction of different branches of state policy, such as immigration and child welfare, also has harmful impacts on children. Together with Migrant Children is an organisation that supports migrant children in the UK who have little or no access to support from their local council, including for medical care. Its director, Nick Watts, shares experiences of working with families who are 'treated like a burden' by local authorities. While the Children Act states that all children are entitled to welfare, Nick explains that families with No Recourse to Public Funds due to their immigration status can be denied necessary care for their children, such as disability support. He says that it sometimes feels like, 'Children have rights, but only if they have the right papers.'

Child welfare services also work closely with the police and criminal justice system. Mandatory reporting mechanisms mean that social workers act as a bridge to the prison system for vulnerable people. These jobs are so closely interlinked that as austerity cuts have impacted social services, pressure has been put on police to step in to provide many of the care duties usually covered by social workers and mental health crisis teams. Even in the state's view, social care provides the same functions as police control with a kinder face; whether the state labels us 'vulnerable' or 'criminal', our treatment and our place in society is much the same.

Racism is often a determining factor in the state's judgements about 'fitness for parenting'. Moreover, job regulations restrict social workers from building truly trusting relationships with families and children. PREVENT legislation requires social workers to monitor the people they are supposed to support for signs of beliefs that 'oppose fundamental British values'. The criteria given for these 'signs' are vague at best and create an avenue for Muslim and South Asian families to be targeted for home searches and arrests. Sex workers or people engaged in other criminalised activities to make money also risk losing their children. Social workers are mandated to report their 'concerns' to the police, eroding any reasons for their clients to open up to them. This is not to say there are not well-meaning social workers who are trying their best within a punishing system, but the job has become ingrained with saviourism and surveillance.

Over half of the young people in prison right now have been through the care system, and many will continue to be imprisoned as adults, disappearing from society for most of their lives. It's time to build new systems that strengthen our communities, rather than deplete them.

8.

LESSONS IN PUNISHMENT

School can be a stepping stone to 'success', or it can be a trapdoor to the prison system—more often than not, we're not the ones in control of which it will be. Our society propagates the lie that social mobility can be achieved through education, when instead, elite universities maintain a hierarchical world where knowledge and information are hoarded behind journal paywalls and in private libraries. Scoring highly in exams and degrees is supposed to push young people up the ladder into 'good jobs', but the fact is that only 4% of people in Britain earn more than £46,000 per year. The maths of social mobility just doesn't add up. In reality, your class position is largely determined by the wealth and status of your parents. Most well-off people don't actually have 'dream jobs'—instead, they own things and tend to already be rich and privileged. The social aim of our education system is really to enforce society's racialised class structure as it is, not to spread knowledge or lift working-class kids to new heights. After all, you can read, study, write and think anywhere.

Over centuries of colonialism, the British education system has been exported all over the world and is considered a major draw for many migrant families to the UK. But schools have long been used by British imperialists in the USA, Canada and Australia as tools to cut Indigenous children off from their communities, cultures and languages. Meanwhile in Britain, caning and other forms of physical punishment were only abolished in schools in 1986, and not until 1999 in independent schools. Even afterwards, corporal punishment remained a very controversial issue, with many teachers arguing it was necessary for discipline. The punitive methods seen in prisons are mirrored in our education system, with the state and society labelling people as criminals right from childhood.

With caning off the table, schools turned to isolation and exclusion as their go-to means of exerting control over their students. School exclusions (suspensions and expulsions), pupil referral units (known as PRUs, these are highly securitised institutions for children who have been permanently excluded from school), and plans to name new children's prisons 'secure schools' are all reforms of a historically violent system. The most common reason for school exclusion is 'disruptive behaviour', an extremely vague category that can mean anything from the appearance of not listening, to doodling, to laughing 'too loudly'. Studies have shown that children from racialised communities, as well as poor and/or disabled children, are most likely to be labelled as disruptive. It's not news that a racist, classist and ableist education system thinks of children from these backgrounds as inherently less capable, trustworthy and well behaved. But to label children as problematic, disruptive or dangerous from such a young age has life-long social, mental and economic consequences.

Kadeem was first expelled at the age of six. The headteacher 'disliked' him—a six-year-old child. He was removed from mainstream education by the age of nine, and by ten he had been held in a PRU and in mental health detention. Despite various disability diagnoses, his learning was utterly unsupported throughout his entire battle with the education system, and his care was passed on to so many different boroughs that his current GP has no record of fifteen years of his medical history. Being one of only a few students in 'alternative provision' to get enough GCSEs to go on to further education, by the time he entered mainstream college, Kadeem suffered from such low self-esteem that he felt he would never belong in mainstream education and was unable to complete his studies. He was later arrested outside his home and spent eight days in prison on remand, with no chance to explain his disabilities or his needs. Kadeem was remanded because he was deemed 'high risk', in part due to his history of school exclusion. He feels that the plainclothes police officer, who didn't identify himself, used his race as a Black person, his class background and his disabilities to criminalise him. This trauma continues to impact him and his ability to place trust in institutions meant to support his care. Kadeem's experiences led him to join No More Exclusions, part of a growing resistance to the exclusion-to-prison pipeline in the UK.

Sumayyah's son Elliot is another young, disabled, Black person, whose experience similarly highlights the power that schools wield in children's lives. Elliot was excluded from mainstream schooling and provided with no alternative means to access education. Sumayyah started her own informal school at home for Elliot and other disabled children who had been excluded, and she launched a legal challenge against the council's negligence. Elliot was taken into foster care to punish both him and his mother.

One member of lCFree, a youth-led campaign in South London fighting racism in schools and on the streets, was violently arrested at the age of fourteen after an Islamophobic neighbour called the police on a family party. When she went back to school after spending the night in a police cell, she was interrogated by school staff as to whether she had committed a crime. School should have been a safe haven for her. Instead of receiving emotional support from staff for the distressing experience of assault and imprisonment by the police, she was met with pointed fingers.

Black Caribbean children are five times as likely to be excluded from school as white children, and more than half of boys in young offenders institutions are from Black and Minority Ethnic backgrounds. Experiences of exclusion are often followed by criminalisation. Labelled as a criminal by society since childhood, young people find that the trapdoor to prison opens and there is rarely a way out.

New 'secure school' child imprisonment facilities will be overseen by both the Department for Education and the Crown Prosecution Service, blending schooling with prisons. 'School-based police officers' are becoming more common, resulting in the harassment of young people in a space meant for learning, part of which is about making mistakes. As reported by Kids of Colour, Black students at Wright Robinson College in Manchester shared that they faced particular surveillance and discrimination by the police officer at their school; one child was forced to show what they had dropped on the floor—a lip balm—since the officer believed it to be cannabis. Marginalised children are also likely to have their issues at school escalated to the criminal justice system or other external agencies, such as social workers and housing officers. This potential for data-sharing, under the guise of building community safety, creates a web of surveillance that impacts vulnerable children from a young age. The state stalks, harasses and abuses these children, then gaslights and blames them when they find themselves traumatised and homeless, unemployed or in prison.

One of the first lessons the education system teaches us is about punishment. The second is about our place in society.

9.

WORKER EXPLOITATION

We aren't going to be able to create our vision of a new world if we're trapped under the grinding wheel of capitalist exploitation. Under capitalism, land and capital are owned privately, instead of commonly by the people. Land is the earth, water and natural resources of our planet, while capital means all assets that can be used to produce more wealth: money, tools, property, machinery. Under capitalism, the ruling classes own and control everything, while the working classes are exploited: we must trade our labour, time, energy, skills, ideas and health for money in order to pay for the things that we need to live. In a capitalist economy, profit accumulation by the ruling classes is valued over the wellbeing of people and communities.

Those without capital who don't work are punished with poverty, and then further punished for being poor. But despite needing to work to live, some people, such as migrants, are legally prevented from working, and certain types of work are criminalised.

It's all exploitation, and it has a long history. Europeans, including the British, colonised the world centuries ago to extract resources and labour from communities in the Global South. This colonial relationship of extraction is replicated today through processes of globalisation and the interconnectedness of trade and finance. In the 1980s, Margaret

Thatcher and Ronald Reagan ushered in the era of neoliberalism, or extreme free-market capitalism, through privatisation, austerity—cutting public funds and services—and deregulation. We are still fighting the consequences. A system that requires and thrives off inequality is justified through the beloved conservative idea that with hard work and personal responsibility, anyone can work their way up. But we know just as well as they do that this is a lie—if the hardest-working people in this country were the wealthiest, the income pyramid would be upside down. The truth is that wealth concentrated at the top never trickles down to the rest of us.

Like those of us outside prison, our communities behind bars have to pay to live. Basic necessities, including toothpaste and food items, are not provided by the prison and are marked up by private companies who operate the canteen. People inside are also exploited as workers, under oppressive conditions in which they can be disciplined or sent to solitary confinement for refusing work, even for medical or religious reasons. There are no sick days or breaks in prison jobs. Low wages and high profit are the theme of exploitation, both inside and outside prison; in 2020, the minimum wage for working imprisoned people was £4 a week. You can't include this 'work experience' on your CV to find a job once you get released. You can't quit, go on strike, ask for a higher wage, organise in a union, or take many of the actions used by unions on the outside without risking solitary confinement, transfer further away from your loved ones, or even abuse.

By joining forces in labour unions, workers can build bargaining power through their ability to withhold their labour in strike actions. This means they can negotiate with employers for better pay and working conditions for everyone. 'Without strong collective bargaining power, raising salaries—especially in private companies—is an impossible task,' explains an anonymous Trades Union Congress member. But ever since Thatcher's leadership, government and business have worked together to deregulate the workplace, reducing both the reach and the impact of trade unions across the UK since the mass strike actions in the 1970s and 1980s. In 2020, about 6.56 million people in Britain were trade union members—compare that to 12.2 million in 1980. According to the Office for National Statistics, the year 2017 counted the lowest number of strike actions since records began in 1891. 'The decrease in union membership just increases the income disparity between middle and high earners, proving money is getting directed to profits rather than wages or quality,' says the TUC trade unionist.

There are many barriers to organising in the workplace, including lack of public awareness about what unions can do, and the compounding impacts of poverty, discrimination and austerity. Workers who unionise can face serious threats to their livelihoods, freedom and personal safety, such as violence, arrest, blacklisting and being fired. These barriers discourage collective action—workers want to avoid losing their pay and are moved instead to think and work individualistically. This is a crisis in the fight against capitalist exploitation.

10.

AN ABLEIST SOCIETY

When Elliot discovered his sister would be leaving their shared home due to an ongoing custody battle, he responded just as any fourteen-year-old boy in distress might—he had a meltdown. His mum, Sumayyah, a community care activist, had popped out to their local shop when she received a terrifying phone call. Elliot is Black and autistic and lived in a rural white area, where instead of meeting his emotional distress with empathy and care, his neighbours had called the police. Despite Sumayyah's pleas, six police officers entered their home and violently restrained Elliot. One officer smashed Sumayyah's phone when she tried to call an ambulance for her son. Elliot spat at him and was subsequently charged with assaulting three police officers.

In a carceral state, disabled people, particularly Black disabled people, are excluded from mainstream education, removed from their homes and communities, institutionalised and criminalised for needing support. As Sumayyah tells us, for disabled people, 'There's no safe space—someone's always policing you, and they're not necessarily the police.'

The medical and cultural mainstream represent disability as a biological abnormality that requires treatment to fix. These ideas about defectiveness and the need to be cured are predicated on the notion of a superior, 'normal' body (read:

white, slim and able-bodied) and are informed by the same logics of disposability that are used to construct the 'criminal'. In an individualised society that tethers our survival to what we can produce, disabled people are marked as failed subjects, justifying the violence of forced treatment, denial of bodily autonomy and infantilisation at the hands of the medical industrial complex. This contemporary abuse of disabled people is rooted in a history of British colonial violence and eugenics that produced and reproduced binaries of able/disabled, well/unwell and normal/abnormal, which worked to dehumanise and eradicate certain people. This system of organised punitive violence against disabled people is called ableism. It is a system that values bodies according to white-supremacist standards and seeks to regulate and control individuals in order to fix society's problems, and it is critical to the functioning of prisons.

Ableism helps us to understand why, at the age of seventeen, Elliot was sentenced to six months in prison as a punishment for exhibiting distress whilst living in supported accommodation. It sheds light on the death of Annabella Landsberg, a Black, disabled woman living with diabetes and HIV, at HMP Peterborough in 2016, after she was denied food and medication and was forcibly restrained by four prison officers. It explains why Metropolitan Police officer Benjamin Kemp beat a seventeen-year-old Black girl with learning difficulties thirty-four times with his baton after she flagged his car down for assistance in 2021. Or why early fears about Covid-19 were soothed by the revelation that the elderly and those with pre-existing conditions were most at risk of dying from the virus. A mere decade after a BBC *Panorama* investigation in 2011 exposed the horrifying institutional abuse against neurodivergent and intellectually disabled people at Winterbourne View hospital, data from the Office for National Statistics showed that disabled people made up 60% of Covid-19 deaths in England in 2020, with the highest rates being in nursing and care homes.

The Tory government may point to our social care system and free NHS as testament to the support available to disabled people in the UK, but it cannot be ignored that William Beveridge, credited with the conceptualisation of the post-war welfare state, was a notorious eugenicist. Ableism, therefore, has been baked into the system responsible for our care from its very beginnings. The Department for Work and Pensions imposes benefit sanctions on disabled people for arbitrary violations such as missing a phone call, and common mistakes, like forgetting to inform the government about changes in your circumstances, are punishable by prison. Disability benefits and support have gradually been decimated in Austerity Britain, whilst the general public is encouraged to surveil and report 'benefit scroungers' for the supposed protection of our underfunded public services. This is not even to mention that access to the meagre support available to disabled people is dependent on divulging private and sensitive information. Moreover, disabled and fat people are routinely gaslighted and abused by ableist doctors, which can translate to having their children taken into care or being denied eligibility to adopt. This control over access to parenting echoes the eugenicist sterilisation of deviant bodies across history.

In fact, during the Covid-19 pandemic, our highly valorised NHS instructed its staff to issue do-not-resuscitate orders for disabled people, as they were not seen as worth the resources. 'Disabled people have their personal autonomy taken away from them. Disability is a failing of ourselves, therefore we are not valid enough to be able to judge what is happening within our bodies in the way that other people are,' says community activist Eshe Kiama Zuri. 'I say, I need this, this, this and this to be able to survive, and they're like, well, we'll give you half of this, and now you must be eternally grateful to me, because the NHS is free and we could just leave you to die, and we're not doing that.'

But in practice, our medical institutions are doing exactly that—leaving people to die—as the carceral state continues its cycle of abandonment and abuse of disabled people.

11.

THE MENTAL HEALTH INDUSTRIAL COMPLEX

It is easy to think that mental health awareness has been achieved, as we see the spread of government-backed adverts reminding us that 'every mind matters'. But these empty 'mental health' campaigns are used to reassure the public that help is available if we just 'speak up'. The ongoing expansion of the Serenity Integrated Mentoring (SIM) system across the NHS, which assigns police officers to patients experiencing mental health crises so as not to 'waste' NHS resources, highlights how measures to normalise mental health treatment are largely removed from the reality of living with mental illness in Britain. Those diagnosed with less palatable mental health issues, like personality disorders or psychosis, are still scapegoated as dangers to society and criminalised. Mental health services have been gutted and replaced with policing and detainment, as vulnerable people continue to be funnelled into prisons that cause even more trauma.

In 2016, Sarah Reed, a Black woman, died awaiting a psychiatric evaluation while on remand at Holloway Prison. An inquest concluded that unacceptable delays and failures in her psychiatric care had contributed to her death. While Sarah may have died in prison, we cannot ignore that she was first sent there for having defended herself against sexual assault in a psychiatric hospital. It becomes clear that funding mental health services will not itself prevent harm when these services are functions of the same carceral state that disregards healing and measures wellness by our 'fitness to work'. Mental health services are not just letting people down; they are actively causing harm.

The Western mental health industrial complex depoliticises mental health according to a normative standard of wellness within white and able-bodied presentation. Within these constructs, people are perceived as healthy as long as they are able to work and reproduce capitalism. Madness is perceived as a deficient biological state to be cured by expert psychiatrists, who once promoted lobotomies and who have long pathologised 'deviant' gender expressions and sexual identities. We know that there is no universal way to respond to distress; the concepts of mental health and illness have always been debated and are still misunderstood, with the Diagnostic and Statistical Manual of Mental Disorders ever changing.

Amal, a member of QueerCare, a transfeminist community care collective, shares with us their impressions of how these narratives impact mad people's treatment. 'Take things like hearing voices,' they say. 'Ableist narratives and psychiatry tell us that if someone's hearing voices or is perceiving a different reality to people around them, then that must mean that they're going to be dangerous. There's no considering that maybe, that person's experience and the way that they're interacting with the world around them, that's actually making things a lot more bearable. Or there's other reasons behind it. Just because it's not what's considered the norm, doesn't mean it's inherently dangerous, but it leads to people being criminalised.'

Under Section 136 of the Mental Health Act, police are granted the right to detain people in distress, a process commonly known as sectioning. When sectioned, people are removed from their communities and involuntarily confined, often indefinitely, in psychiatric hospitals, where they are denied all agency, restrained, and forced either to take medications to incapacitate them or to risk being labelled non-compliant—all under the guise of care. As Amal states, 'Psychiatry is intimately connected with incarceration, most obviously through sectioning, a form of medical incarceration, but also in the way that it legitimises other forms of incarceration.' An example of this was the 'Dangerous and Severe Personality Disorder' Programme, introduced by New Labour in the early 2000s to 'preventatively' detain people considered a high risk to society as a way to funnel more funding into prisons. Although this was never a medically supported diagnosis and is no longer in use today, the policy's impacts are lasting; most prisons still have special 'offender personality disorder units', and people are routinely denied parole because they have been diagnosed with a disordered personality.

Our social conditioning plays a huge role in determining how we respond when we witness someone in crisis. Do we fear a perceived violent individual or see someone in pain who needs care and empathy? Because of this conditioning, our ideas about safety and risk can be difficult to disentangle from the punitive culture around us. Often, reasonable responses to trauma and oppression are pathologised by the medical establishment. Our discomfort with and collective inability to respond to madness legitimises the carceral state, as the health-care system tells us that some bodies need to be controlled. When mental health professionals are positioned as authorities over our own minds, we stop feeling responsible towards each other's care and instead learn to respond to each other's pain by calling the authorities.

The carceral state puts us through poverty, surveillance, coercive control, dehumanisation and brutality and then leaves us to rely on the same institutions that are destroying us to administer our care. It determines which minds matter and which do not. Madness is viewed as a deviation from the norm, and the mental health industrial complex justifies the subjection of certain bodies to state violence.

Ultimately, we don't know for sure what causes madness or mental distress, but we do know that if you're homeless, or unable to afford food, or trapped in an abusive situation, it's going to have a significant impact on your mental wellbeing. Yet the mental health industrial complex removes the structural context of harm from its assessment of our health. We are living with the ongoing legacies of colonialism, as well as with a daily onslaught of systemic discrimination. But as we try to live in a world built to destroy us, our survival mechanisms are medicalised, and we are criminalised and punished for the ways we try to cope with our traumas.

12.

THE GENDER BINARY

As nonbinary artist Jacob V. Joyce tells us, 'The existence of trans people presents a threat to one of the central tenets of the white-supremacist, capitalist state—that we all need to just accept our place within its violent system.' From birth, we are coercively assigned a place in a rigid system of gendered categorisation, which polices our actions and controls our bodies. To some cis people held captive by this binary, the root of patriarchal violence is in 'male biology', while the category of womanhood is defined by suffering and subjection to pain. Trans people's counter-conception of gender as a joyful and imaginative experience rattles these 'trans-exclusionary radical feminists' or TERFs, for whom gender is simply indicative of one's biologically assigned position in a hierarchy of violence.

The gender binary is a racialised social construct with roots in British colonialism, which erased Indigenous systems of gender, criminalised homosexuality and punitively enforced the notion of gender as determined by immutable biological sex. The same mechanisms, language and frameworks that are used to police trans people's bodies work to oppress all marginalised women, especially Black women. Activist Sami recognises gender as 'an enforced categorisation process, used to punish and to create systems of punishment.' Deviation from these norms leads to punishment, which 'creates the power imbalances that are then exploited by the carceral system.' This is how the gender binary is used to make the world into a prison.

In recent years, the vicious current of transphobia across British mainstream media has revealed that the liberal goal of trans visibility does not deliver meaningful or material change for most trans people; in fact, visibility is weaponised by the carceral state to further police and punish. Transphobia plays an enormous role in legitimising the actions of the carceral state, as fearmongering about trans women using women's spaces, including women's prisons, provide cover for the real threat to women's safety and rights: decades of austerity, under-funded women's services and a violent state. In 2020, Women and Equalities Minister Liz Truss abandoned plans to reform the 2004 Gender Recognition Act, preserving the medicalisation of trans identity rather than giving trans people the most basic rights to self-identification. It is not surprising that in her former role as justice secretary, Truss planned huge expansions to the prison estate.

The reality is that trans people—particularly trans people of colour, disabled trans people and trans sex workers—face especially high rates of criminalisation, surveillance and state violence. At least nine trans women have died in prison since 2007, according to the Bent Bars Project. Prisons exemplify gender as a system of social stratification. Behind prison bars, trans people are removed from their communities, held captive in dehumanising conditions organised by gender categories imposed at birth, subjected to horrific abuse, and kept isolated in vulnerable prisoner units, whilst being denied access to gender-affirming healthcare.

The routine sexual violence exerted by the state against trans people extends well beyond the confines of the prison. Driven by scarcity politics that tells us we need to restrict access to support services to even fewer women, rape crisis centres are encouraged to screen for and avoid supporting trans women.

Further, trans people in the UK face medical abuse at the hands of a structurally exclusionary NHS that denies trans people bodily autonomy and acts as a gatekeeper to healthcare. Transphobia has recently manifested in unfounded fears, stoked by the media, that children must be protected from coercive transition and puberty blockers; in actual fact, young trans people unable to access these life-affirming medical treatments have a staggeringly high suicide rate.

While trans life is under constant threat, the British media floods us with pointless debates around whether the trans community are lobbying for a gender-neutral Mr Potato Head. These unproductive conversations are deliberately designed to keep us distracted from the constructs that sustain the state's violence. For writer and educator Fopé Ajanaku, drawing attention to the arbitrary cruelty of the gender binary would cause people to question 'what else underpins the mechanisms of oppression in the world.' They would begin to ask, 'How does capital work? How does money work? How does race work? How does class work? Once you have to unpick it, you have to unpick everything. The question then is, what's at stake? What's the cost here? And the conclusion is that the cost is too high, so they're more willing to police gender identity than to deal with anything else.'

13.

RAPE CULTURE

It's hard to name violence when it happens. Our patriarchal culture excuses violence, minimises it, makes it seem like it's 'not a big deal'. A lot of us have experiences of being blamed for something that's happened to us, because we were 'asking for it' in some way, or of not being believed because the person who harmed us just 'doesn't seem like that kind of person'.

When a person is sexually violated, it is usually by someone they know. Most sexual assault is perpetrated by partners, exes, dates, friends and work colleagues—people we are likely to trust to some degree. According to government statistics, in 2017–2020, less than 1 in 6 rape victims in England and Wales reported their experience to the police. Of cases that were reported in 2020, only 1.6% ended in a suspect being charged. Even fewer perpetrators receive a conviction. Throughout that long, drawn-out process, a person is forced to preserve their body like a crime scene rather than being able to wash and tend to themself, to relive the details of their trauma multiple times with police, lawyers and judges, and to have their relationships, behaviour and experiences picked apart in court. Even if a conviction is reached, the system does not put in place any safety measures to support someone who is still traumatised when the process is over, as though there can be a time limit on their pain. And in the vast majority of instances, cases are not brought to trial, which can be a seriously invalidating experience when we are told the 'right' thing to do when we are harmed—to keep other people safe and to find justice—is to go to the police and try to get someone sent to prison. As people against all sexual assault, abuse and coercive control, we reject the idea that we must rely on a system that enacts that same violence on any of us.

Abolition feminism follows in the legacy of Black revolutionaries like Angela Davis and Mariame Kaba, challenging us to imagine beyond prisons and police as we seek solutions to the rampant domestic and sexual violence in our society. It is a movement led by and for those of us who experience violence at the hands of both the state and people in our communities; those who worry about the consequences for ourselves and our loved ones if we call the police; those whose work is criminalised and whose traumas are turned against us; those unable to leave our abusers without becoming homeless; those unable to call for help for fear of deportation.

The figure of the rapist—terrifying, violent and uncontrollable—is so repulsive that we cannot bear to think any of our loved ones might be capable of such an act. We want to distance ourselves, as 'normal' people, as far from that behaviour as possible; we convince ourselves that surely no one that *we* know would do such a thing. We are also comforted by the notion of the rapist as an unknown monster that jumps out of the bushes at night, because it means we don't have to address the violence happening right in front of us. And for those of us who are vulnerable to that violence, we internalise these narratives about danger, grasping for ways to keep ourselves safe in situations we are told are most risky.

'You really are taught to imagine that sexual violence is something that happens in specific circumstances to specific people, and not something that's embedded in our gender relations and how we conceptualise masculinity. Our society is organised around sexual violence.' Lola Olufemi, Black feminist writer and organiser, shares her insight with us. 'In a society that's organised around the exploitation of huge numbers of people, it follows that yes, sexual violence then becomes something so common, because it is another expression of exploitation, of domination.'

Rape is built into our culture, and the state's carceral responses put our people at risk of other kinds of harm. Indeed, police officers are often abusive themselves. From 2019 to 2021, at least 129 women made reports of domestic abuse by partners in the police, and people working as sex workers told us they had been sexually assaulted by police officers, leaving them with no one they could report the harm to. The prison system is also unable to address deep issues of power abuse in our society and communities. Over half of the people held in women's prisons have experienced abuse—so how does our society contend with someone being both a survivor and a criminal?

The Sarah Reed Campaign for Justice is led by the family members of one survivor who died in state custody. The campaign has gained national attention for the ways it spotlights not just the failings but also the active violence of the state when it comes to the care of criminalised vulnerable people. Sarah Reed, a Black, working-class woman who was mentally unwell and traumatised, was not protected by her web of social workers, psychiatrists or police. She had been physically assaulted by a police officer and was later sexually assaulted in a psychiatric institution. For defending herself against her attacker, she was sent to HMP Holloway, where she ultimately tragically died. Prisons do not protect us from violence; they enact it. Every day, the police and prison officers assault people through strip searches, physical restraint and brutality. We cannot rely on a patriarchal criminal justice system that solves problems through control, coercion and violence—the very behaviours from which we need protection.

The carceral state is designed only to deal with the aftermath of sexual violence, not prevention. Sexual violence services are mostly funded by the criminal justice system and are geared primarily toward supporting survivors through their experience of reporting crime. Only rarely are police called in the moment itself, perhaps in life-threatening situations of domestic violence. Yet in England and Wales alone, two women are still murdered by a partner or an ex every week. According to Rape Crisis, around one incident of serious sexual assault is happening per hour in England and Wales. Ninety per cent of rapes are perpetrated by someone known to the person being harmed—not by strangers, as we are often led to believe. Even though many of us are warned against walking down empty streets at night, home is often the most dangerous place for us to be.

If the system imprisoned every perpetrator of a sexual offence to the maximum extent of the law, the courts would be backlogged for decades. Almost 100,000 people experience what are considered the most serious types of sexual offences every year, according to Rape Crisis, but fewer than 1,000 cases result in a charge or court summons. The courts are already backlogged dealing with other—less harmful—kinds of 'crime'. The criminal justice system is not truly concerned with dealing with the scale of the problem of sexual violence, and it is vital that our imaginations not be limited by the false promises it presents. Prisons are not here to protect us from rapists. Prisons exist to protect the status quo, and that includes rape culture.

For as long as our ideas of safety and justice are wrapped up in imprisonment and punishment, we will continue to justify the expansion of the criminal justice system and border regime and their entanglement with the services we access to seek care and support. When someone wants to leave a violent relationship but has nowhere to go, the National Domestic Abuse Helpline connects them to the refuge system, a housing network for survivors with support workers on site. This housing can create a lifeline for many of the women it serves, yet it relies on isolation as a safety mechanism, as survivors abandon their homes and communities to move to a secretly located house with other people who often are not getting adequate support for their trauma. It is an emergency response, because we have no wider infrastructure in our communities for intervening in or healing from harm. In state-regulated refuge housing, you have a curfew and restrictions on whom you can see and what you can do. These services consult with other state agencies, including the police, before providing housing. Many survivors end up feeling that control over their lives has merely transitioned from their abuser to the state. No one deserves to be scrutinised when they are asking for help.

We speak to Ivié Itoje, who works within the women's sector supporting Black and brown survivors of violence. She is critical of the role that state services can play in reducing violence. 'When you see the practices of the Home Office and the police, it's alarming to me that we would think that the same people actively promoting state-sanctioned abuse would then see it as necessary to reduce it. It doesn't even add up.' Racism is built into this system, and it plays out in police responses when survivors do call emergency services. 'White men don't even get like, a tap on the wrist from the police,' Ivié relates to us. 'In fact, it's the women that end up bearing the brunt and losing their children to these horrible people. Whereas with Black women that are in relationships with Black men, I don't even think what's happening is seen as serious at all.' In her experience of frontline work and in her community, Ivié says that women of colour, especially darker-skinned Black women and South Asian women, are more likely to be considered the 'perpetrator' if the police are called, and to end up in prison themselves. This has certainly been the case with one of our friends imprisoned in the South of England, a Black woman and former sex worker who is serving an indefinite IPP sentence after being punched by a client and then arrested.

Symbolic solutions to gender-based violence offered by the government, such as proposals to make misogyny into a hate crime, only serve to expand the carceral state. This kind of legislation allows the state to define misogyny as between individuals, hiding the causes and context of misogyny and the violence that the state perpetrates against women.

In London, the Mayor's Office for Police and Crime (MOPAC) and the Home Office have played key roles in shaping legislation around gender-based violence, such as the Domestic Abuse Bill and the Police, Crime, Sentencing and Courts Bill. These bills have focused on increasing prison sentences and granting more power to the police, the courts and parole boards, with no commitment to funding communities to support each other. Such legislative moves are driven by the desire to imprison more people and increase state control over all of our lives, not to reduce violence.

Ivié explains, 'There's a lack of critique as to why the police are coming to you to supposedly reduce domestic violence. Is it more control, is it to get more people on the radar, to see how many undocumented migrants are out there?' Evidently, this has been the impact, with more people in prison and detention than ever before while rates of violence have remained the same, if not become higher. Under austerity and the hostile environment, our only legal avenues for support have been cut. Domestic violence services for women of colour are having to turn away 2 out of 3 people who come to them for help. It leaves too many with nowhere to go.

14.

COPAGANDA

PC Yasmin 'Yaz' Khan in cult classic BBC show *Doctor Who* is well equipped to use her investigative skills to take on the role as the first South Asian companion to the Doctor. In a flashback, young Yaz is sitting by a country road, considering running away from home, when a police officer, a middle-aged white woman, approaches her. The officer has been to Yaz's mum's house and knows she's been having a hard time at home. Yaz is comforted by the officer's kind reassurance—she too felt like giving up, she says, but those moments have always passed. The officer strikes a bet with Yaz that in three years everything will be different, and Yaz accepts. Sure enough, Yaz is now a police officer too and a member of Team TARDIS and looking back on the memory of the officer who saved her.

Positive portrayals of police on TV contribute to the story in our society that police exist to help people—a key reason why lots of people are attracted to joining the police force. We can't ignore the narratives told about safety, harm and the police when we think about what we need to dismantle to build an abolitionist vision. It is important to unpick common tales of the hero versus the villain and good versus evil, and to think about who's benefiting from these narratives. When pro-police storylines become a central theme in our entertainment, it is often called 'copaganda'. We spoke to eight producers and political commentators on the impact of copaganda across UK media.

Micha Frazer-Carroll, cultural and political journalist and writer, reflects on how pieces she's written about copaganda have been received: '"It doesn't have to be realistic, we just want to enjoy things," is what people comment usually.' But whether we're watching for escapism or realism, it's worth interrogating why police are the protagonists in so many of the most popular primetime programmes, and what impact these depictions have on our perception of them.

'I used to think that police operated in quite mystical ways, with all the tech they have,' says Micha. 'But now I know that's not how it works at all.' We are definitely being misled when shows such as *Line of Duty*, whose Season Six finale attracted an average of around 12.8 million viewers, show off technology and surveillance equipment available to the police and lead viewers to believe that these tools are used against police corruption. Facial recognition technology and body-worn cameras are far more frequently used for the criminalisation and racist treatment of low-income communities than to keep police in check.

In media and entertainment, we are often exposed to harmful tropes that attempt to 'tick the box' for representation, such as characters assumed to be trans women and sex workers handcuffed in the background in police stations, or groups of Black people assumed to be drug dealers. The stories that are told over and over are of oppressed people suffering, struggling with their identities and trying to fit in the status quo. Our fight is about more than seeing people we relate to on screen; it's to end the racist, pro-police propaganda we are fed every day.

Individuals who gain access to writers' rooms may not all be aware of the cultural power they have, but they are still positioned to reinforce a norm that maintains the state's right to use violence. British drill artists Skengdo and AM were sentenced to a nine-month suspended sentence in 2019 simply for performing their music. While young Black people are criminalised for 'inciting violence' when they tell stories through music on YouTube, the same cannot be said for those who create media that encourages people to join the police. Black and brown artists and activists who build a following frequently experience censorship and 'shadow banning', which limits their reach online or outright removes them from social media platforms. Many of these platforms simultaneously host a slew of far-right, eugenicist, queerphobic and racist content, which is much less policed.

Copaganda not only reproduces pro-police narratives, but it also reinforces notions of criminality. Jenny has worked as an assistant producer on a few crime dramas in her career and explains, 'It's very much, "This person is a criminal, because they have some kind of personal flaw."' These, too, are one-dimensional depictions of characters, which fail to represent the complexities of our world. Meanwhile, when police characters are also depicted as having a history of criminality, we view their crime differently to criminals' crime. Often, these detectives and cops will be permitted a flaw. Have a think about how many series you've watched where our hero has an addiction, is violent, or has an unfortunate need or desire to commit murder. We extend our empathy to the hero, but we stop there.

Abolition requires us to question the narratives we absorb about who commits crime or harm: the disposability of villains and criminals is stark in our current oversimplified visions of 'justice'. Slamming a big door on the baddie in their cell might offer an audience a sense of conclusion, but problems aren't so simply disposed of in real life.

Abolition also requires us to take responsibility for each other, and not to simply wait for a hero to save us. Jenny explains that producers feed exceptional characteristics to writers, asking, 'How can we make this character stand out from the crowd?' She points out that detectives on TV are set up not to be like normal people. 'Therefore, when they do act differently, we think, oh, that's because he's Sherlock or whoever. That's not what I can do.'

Awate, a grassroots activist and artist, tells us about how police were depicted in early Hollywood as slapstick characters. In silent comedy films produced by Mack Sennett between 1912 and 1917, the Keystone Cops were an incompetent police force ridiculed as 'enemies of the working class'. Awate explains that as the industry of celebrity grew and film studios' crew members began to be targeted by police for their involvement with drug use or because of homophobic laws, 'Deals were struck with studios to protect their stars and writers from being arrested. In exchange, they were going to let police input in the shows. Police will lend them cars, give them advice, and work in their propaganda.'

A hundred years later, the entertainment industry is built on strict hierarchies controlled by money and privilege. The power of fame, especially for white cis men, protects people from the consequences of causing harm. For marginalised people in the industry, exploitation continues. Women of colour, for example, are frequently blacklisted if they speak out against power abuse and discrimination in their industry. When sexual harassment, assault and coercion are tools deployed to maintain the structures of the entertainment industry itself, it continues to favour the industry to have the police and the entire prison industrial complex on side. What better way to do that than to cast your cops as heroes?

There are some who are working to challenge those structures and thinking about collective ownership over media. Siân Robins-Grace, who co-produced Netflix hit *Sex Education*, poses the question: 'Would we ever have a production where the director would get paid the same amount as the runner?' Power imbalances behind the scenes are reflected in the narratives we see on screen. The world that is presented to us neither reflects the world we currently live in nor the world that could be the site of our liberation. The conditions under which we produce stories, the exploitation and the gatekeeping, are squashing our imaginations and suppressing our ability to tell new stories about our collective power.

3.

BRICK BY BRICK: THE BUILDING

Evoking the legacy of W.E.B. Du Bois, we argue that dismantling systems of racism, sexism and oppression will not result in chaos; rather, it will give us the space, time and resources to reconstruct the world that we all deserve. There is pragmatic, strategic abolitionist work being done right now to dismantle the systems of policing, surveillance and imprisonment that span the globe. Abolitionist work can and should resist every point at which the criminal justice system interlocks with our lives.

Abolition motivates us to solve problems, instead of attempting to vanish people for being too complicated. We must work to build institutions that affirm our humanity, rather than deny it.

I.

DECOLONISATION AND INTERNATIONAL SOLIDARITY

We follow in the tradition of anti-imperialist and anti-colonial struggle that has been fought for centuries.

Understanding imperial history shows us the importance of international solidarity—we cannot separate what is going on in Palestine now from British history, for example. Imperialism moves beyond borders, and so must we. Social progress for people oppressed under capitalism in the Global North would not have happened without anti-colonial resistance. The British Black Panthers and Claudia Jones were influenced by and collaborated with Black liberation movements in the USA, Haiti and the West Indies. Historically, the struggle against white supremacy, the most destructive and widespread imperial logic in global history, has necessarily been tied to the struggle against apartheid in South Africa and against the Israeli occupation of Palestine.

Western liberalism tricks us into fighting for 'equal rights' within the nation state. But even if we win this fight, the possibility of such a victory hinges on the state's continued extraction and exploitation of people in the Global South. To fight only within the UK's borders would be to continue to further the imperialist cause. We could fight for the much-lauded quality of life and social welfare provision of Scandinavian countries, but these measures too exclude those without the privilege of citizenship, who are still vulnerable to detention and deportation. Moreover, the prosperity of the Scandinavian states relies on the success of militarisation, warfare and the exploitation of labour abroad. We don't want reformed prisons that are maintained on the backs of the oppression of the Global South. We want liberation for all, or none at all.

Defence and Security Equipment International (DSEI) is an international arms fair held every two years at the Excel Centre in London. At this event, heads of brutal states come to hear about and look at the latest tools that companies such as Elbit Systems and BAE Systems have to offer for mass control and termination. This gathering of murderers literally involves strolling around from stall to stall watching videos of drones and tanks being used to kill people in the Middle East to see how effective they are. Whenever DSEI is held, Campaign Against Arms Trade, a coalition of groups working towards the abolition of the international arms trade, gathers outside of the Excel Centre to disrupt the fair, blocking the road, commandeering delivery vehicles and tricking taxis into going to the wrong location.

In solidarity with the struggle to free Palestine from Israeli occupation, organisers have taken to targeting arms factories and office buildings of companies involved in dealing weapons to Israel. Over the course of 2021, Palestine Action and other activists in the UK scaled the roofs of and occupied Elbit Systems' arms factories in Leicester and Tamworth, shutting them down temporarily. The actions were reported to have cost Elbit millions of pounds and gained national media attention, keeping the Palestinian struggle present on our news feeds.

The British state has a history of using violence to suppress anti-colonial dissent. This is also seen in anti-war protests and the aggressive and violent treatment of protesters and activists standing for Palestinian liberation. Expressions of international solidarity have been met with surveillance and the emboldening of police and state powers. The Police, Crime, Sentencing and Courts Bill has been crafted in direct opposition to global solidarity against state oppression and police brutality in the form of widespread protests across the UK in the summer of 2020. Nevertheless, occupations and actions have had more supporters and willing participants recently than they have for decades. The movement is growing.

2.

NO BORDERS, NO NATIONS

Modern global capitalism and histories of colonialism combine to maintain the 'Commonwealth' and Britain's ability to manipulate international institutions such as the United Nations and the World Bank. Taking the form of planned political disruptions, targeted assassinations, sanctions that violate human rights, and the theft of resources from countries in the Global South, Britain's policies fit Huey P. Newton's definition of imperialism. It is a repressive regime that monitors, controls, arrests, detains, incarcerates and deports people all around the world in order to advance the security, wealth and power of the privileged few. It is designed to maintain justice, equity and freedom for these few by oppressing others. As globalisation tips away from Europe and the US, with huge demographic shifts in the Global South and anti-colonial resistance of the status quo taking place on the international stage, we find ourselves living in a moment of great revolutionary potential. At the same time, we have also been witnessing an upsurge in overt xenophobia, right-wing violence and white supremacy, as evidenced in the 2016 Brexit referendum results, and the anti-BLM protests to protect statues of slavers.

Huey P. Newton's theory of intercommunalism helps us to understand the similar positioning of people and communities left behind by deindustrialisation and disadvantaged by the histories of colonialism and imperialism all over the world. Newton argues that global capitalism undermines the four characteristics of an independent nation: economic independence, cultural determination, control of political institutions, and territorial integrity and safety. Imperialism has reduced the vast majority of the world's communities to nation states whose institutions do not serve the interests of the people but rather those of the state and corporations. Furthermore, the impact of the securitisation of borders is both subtle and overt, and it is generally unseen by the general public. As technology advances, so do the methods to create an impenetrable border. The funds pumped into securitisation allow for the use of heat sensors, drones, smart technology and biometrics that encourage 'othering' and criminalise those on the other side of the border. We do not need nation states secured by militaristic border regimes. We need resilient, healthy, interdependent communities.

In the UK, groups such as Lesbians and Gays Support the Migrants and End Deportations have been taking action to intervene on deportation flights taking place on commercial airlines, through online actions, phone blockades and direct action. In March 2017, the notorious Stansted 15 attached themselves to the landing gear of a Titan Airlines plane that had been chartered by the Home Office to deport sixty people to Ghana, Nigeria and Sierra Leone. These protesters were accused of disrupting international air travel and convicted of terrorism-related charges. However, the convictions were overturned on appeal, and none of the Stansted 15 received prison time for their action—an incredible feat of resistance and solidarity. At the time of writing, at least eleven of the people who were due to be deported on that flight are still living in the UK.

Grassroots anti-raids groups have been popping up across the country in response to the government's hostile environment policies. The Anti-Raids Network is a group that got together to create resources to help people know their rights if they see an immigration enforcement officer trying to ask people questions, as they have been known to do outside of stations and at large public events like football matches. Immigration enforcement officers have no more right than anyone else to force a random member of the public to speak to them. Yet, because of these officers' uniform and authoritarian demeanour, many people don't realise that if you are questioned, you can walk right on by.

As well as knowing our rights as individuals, it's important for people to stand together in solidarity to resist the policing of the border. From Haringey, London to Pollokshields, Glasgow, immigration raids at homes and businesses have been blocked by local communities, who swarmed immigration enforcement vans, blocked the streets and resisted until the state's agents gave up and let the people they were attempting to detain go free. Other effective acts of migrant solidarity might include the refusal of people with citizenship to play along with new demands in the health and social care services to present their passports and documents.

By every means possible, it is essential that the impacts of the border on the everyday lives of migrants are opposed and thwarted. Our liberation will not be realised under the constraints and violence of borders. Resistance to migrant oppression and a focus on international solidarity are therefore fundamental to the abolitionist project.

3.

LAND JUSTICE AND REPARATIONS

To build a world without prisons, we need reparations. In the words of land justice organisers Land In Our Names, we must 'seek to disrupt systemic and structural violence of racism and colonialism by conceding power and resources in order to give space, both figuratively and literally, to Black people and People of Colour to repair and heal'. We need space.

We speak to Sam Siva, an organiser with LION, to help shape our understanding of the vision of reparations. Sam explains that while there are people of colour in rural areas of the UK, the areas associated with beauty and the best countryside walks are often occupied by upper-class landowners. With limited public transport links, these spots are hard to reach, and if people of colour from cities do venture out to the countryside, they are confronted with narrow paths, gates to climb over that are not accessible for all bodies, and local residents who are often culturally insensitive.

Reparations ultimately include the relinquishment of the land colonised under the Commonwealth, as well as the redistribution of all money from the monarchy and all the obscured wealth associated with its estate. We must reclaim the land occupied by the Ministry of Justice, such as prisons, courts, police stations and youth offender institutions, land occupied by the Ministry of Defence and the Home Office, and the numerous country estates that have been maintained through wealth accumulated through slavery and colonialism. From Bristol to Glasgow to Belfast to Manchester, the empire built this country from the spoils of the sugar, chocolate and tea trades, and it's time for us to take them back.

Our goals as abolitionists act in parallel with environmental movements that are shining a light on the limitations of the criminal justice system by fighting for corporate accountability. Under national and international legal frameworks that they helped to design, companies responsible for massive ecological devastation, such as catastrophic oil spills or evictions of communities to run pipelines through their land, are not even committing crimes. But they are creating massive, irreversible damage. Prisons and police exist to enable those massive corporate harms in the name of profit, since the people who resist this harm are violently criminalised and displaced.

In the UK, climate justice activists have a long legacy of direct action, engaging a variety of tactics from blocking roads to occupying gas power stations and other powerful acts of civil disobedience. Many of the corporations playing a role in accelerating climate disaster are also the same corporations, or linked to the corporations, that are profiting off prisons and militarisation. We must divest from and ultimately destroy these global corporate powers. We must free our people from the prisons and detention centres that are standing right now and stop them from building any more. We must fight narratives about 'green prisons' and defund and disable all technologies and manifestations of policing, extraction and militarisation, such as police vehicles and equipment used by the fossil fuel industry and the military.

Learning from the tactics used by environmental activists when campaigning against corporate enemies, abolitionists have employed similar ones in campaigns against prison construction and the companies that profit from it. In resistance to the planned construction of the most expensive federal prison in US history, the grassroots collective Fight Toxic Prisons formed, linking environmental justice and abolitionist struggles. FTP fought a five-year campaign alongside environmental activists, local community members, local landowners, students and incarcerated people. Through building unexpected relationships and employing what they call a 'fully fledged diversity of tactics', such as letter-writing, petitions, paperwrenching, legal action and direct action, FTP was able to prolong the planning process of that project until it was no longer financially or politically viable, defeating the prison before it ever even broke ground in 2019. The prison would have been built downstream from a toxic coal slurry impoundment, and less than a mile and a half away from one of the last three untouched stretches of old-growth forest in the state.

Since then, FTP has worked with organisers across Alabama to build the Communities Not Prisons coalition, continuing to apply pressure on private companies that are contracted to build new prisons. In 2021, the CNP coalition successfully forced Barclays to pull out of a huge contract with private-prison profiteer CoreCivic, defeating the Alabama governor's plan to privately build and lease two new mega-prisons in the state.

In London, teenage activists under the collective name Choked Up replaced road signs with warnings that 'BREATHING KILLS' to highlight the punishment they face as a result of air pollution suffered by those living in the poorest areas of the country. Young climate activists in Scotland have begun organising alongside abolitionists to petition against and disrupt the building of mega-prison HMP Glasgow on a site formerly owned by the National Grid. Organisers with Community Action on Prison Expansion (CAPE) have taken on this approach and found environmental grounds to object to each of the new proposed mega-prisons across England and Scotland, such as the destruction of wildlife habitats and contamination to the local water supply. They have also begun to build connections with activists and legal experts to strengthen their struggle.

Relationships of mutual care must extend to our relationships with everything we coexist with on this earth. Liberation means the air we breathe, the water we drink and the delicious food that we eat must not be fraught with exploitation, but rather becomes part of holistic nourishment of our bodies and communities. As we root ourselves in the struggle against empire, we reclaim the land, engaging with and integrating old and new practices and technologies of cultivation and production. We must work at a different pace, a slower one. We must rest. Building a world without prisons requires us to truly commit to deep interdependence and to the repair and transformation of our relationship to the land and its ecosystems.

4.

FOOD JUSTICE

According to Carys Kettlety of National Food Service Bristol, a network of community food projects, we need to 'differentiate between food aid and something transformative and radical.' The latter means building solidarity and autonomous communities, not charity and dependence. The practice of mutual aid is the voluntary exchange of resources and services for collective benefit. Mutual aid is not charity, and it relies only on community. For the National Food Service, the aim is not to simply give people food, but rather to radically change the system that leaves people trapped in food poverty. 'Ownership is a key part of that,' says Carys. 'The space is there to be owned by everyone in the community. Everyone has a say in how it is done.' But funding providers tend to be attracted to bigger food projects, who take a more charity-based approach. 'We are running against the state—we've received loads of referrals from the council but not any funds.'

We have so far to go in creating and rediscovering sustainable ways to grow, harvest, store and share food, and we invite you to join in the brainstorm. What would food justice in Britain look like? In fact, many food justice practices are already going on every day. Guerrilla food production looks like community farms, and projects like the Rose Hill Community Larder in Oxford, which aims to fight food waste, strengthen neighbourhood bonds and make health food affordable. OLIO, a food-sharing app, helps to fight food waste by collecting surplus food from Tesco and allowing people to give away food and household items to neighbours for free. Community fridges are an even simpler alternative. Even something as simple as growing your own herbs or food in your garden or getting your produce from farms and farmer's markets rather than big supermarket chains can be a revolutionary action. By connecting to the land, animals and people around us, we are creating community socialism—providing food and support for each other without violence, profit motive or exploitation of the Global South.

To dream out loud, food justice exists in a world where every child receives a free school meal from someone at school and not a private company. Small farmers and community gardens cultivate and share fresh, locally grown food for free or cheaply. The mass-produced food that we eat is grown by unionised farmers who have a say in what and how they grow, both at home and abroad. The cost of food is not driven up by corporations, who would rather let food spoil than just give it to people; instead, food is managed collaboratively so that the surplus reaches everyone everywhere. After all, the earth is abundant, if we take care of her. This vision is of a post-imperialist world—a globally democratic one where 'free trade' is really freedom from oppression and exploitation. Universal basic income enables us to chase our joy and eat to live. People feel so food-empowered and supported that some choose to grow their own food, raise animals and live off the land. Body positivity is the norm and diets are a strange relic of history. And, from the dreams of National Food Service Bristol, there is at least one community dining centre in every neighbourhood—a social hub where people come together to share free and delicious food.

National Food Service Bristol launched in 2018. Its founding concept is for people to contribute what they can to a democratic community dining space. 'NFS centres are like a living room for the community,' says Carys. 'A place you go to eat with others in your community, not because you can't afford food but because it's nice and the food is lovely.' People contribute in ways that aren't financial, volunteering their time and skills, even washing up or cooking. Each space is different and based on the needs of their communities. There are no barriers between the 'service user' and the 'provider', because all involved are collectively part of the dining experience.

'We started slowly with open meetings and events to gauge the interest and needs in Bristol,' Carys continues. 'We ran an emergency food service for nine months. We served 50,000 meals to 2,500 people over that time in packages, including three days' worth of food and dessert, completely free and not means-tested. We are conscious that we have become a lifeline for people—our closing down took several months, and we have still been supporting some people. We worked with people who are using our service and finding alternatives. We did have to connect them with benefits and also referrals for food banks. There is difficulty in making things "official" at the national level, and we were slow to grow for a few years.'

Carys explains that when the Covid-19 pandemic hit, food insecurity became an increasingly pressing issue for more people across the country. More and more organisations began to join the network. 'However, the administration hadn't caught up to that demand,' says Carys. 'With food delivery slots getting booked quickly, and a lack of access to shops with lockdown, the people receiving our food were primarily single, middle-aged, disabled women.' However, the conversation around food insecurity tends to focus on children and families, such as the government's provision of shoddy free school meal packages over the half-term holiday in autumn 2020. The same had happened earlier in the year, when the Department for Environment, Food and Rural Affairs (through private companies, of course) provided utterly inadequate food parcels to disabled people shielding during the pandemic, all while refusing to support food banks and mutual aid groups.

Communal eating is not historically alien: public kitchens existed in Britain during the interwar period. In this country, the pub used to be the heart of the community, and across the world, communal eating is a key part of maintaining social bonds. The creation of these spaces would bring people together across social boundaries; people would not believe the lies in *The Daily Mail* about their friends in the community. We need to replace alienation and exclusion with communal luxury. It won't be fully democratic or fully perfect, and we can't beat ourselves up if some people do not join. But we must work toward a food justice future that is interconnected with each other and our planet.

5.

HEALTH

An abolitionist approach to our wellbeing is one that is holistic. To abolish the police and the carceral state is to commit to building healthy communities. Our priority is to ease the stress and sickness created by capitalism and oppression. A liberatory approach to health means that when our bodies do need tending to, we can consent to every aspect of our support.

We must decolonise healthcare. The dark colonial histories that built the foundations of biomedical science involve the systematic elimination and devaluation of Indigenous and ancestral treatments and knowledge. The global movement of doulas, for instance, has highlighted many of the practices to support both birth and loss that exist in Black communities and that are being strengthened in resistance to the violence within mainstream healthcare provision. Some of the practices that healers have turned to in the face of medical neglect and distrust in health institutions include herbalism and somatics. Herbalists use plants to make remedies in forms such as balms, tinctures and syrups. Somatics refers to the practice of engaging with the signals of trauma that we carry in our bodies, not just in our minds, from tension in our muscles to tightness in our breath. Somatics practitioners can give us tools to release anger or grief, reduce anxiety and reconnect with our bodies.

Campaigns to disentangle the police and borders from healthcare are fundamental, such as the work of Together with Migrant Children, which advocates for migrant children to receive healthcare that they are frequently denied. Queer people living on the margins also build practical grassroots systems to support each other as an avenue towards harm reduction. These groups experienced the sharp end of state repression in the face of their own health crisis, during the HIV/AIDS pandemic from the 1980s onwards. In response, systems were developed to resist the criminalisation of queer people, sex workers and drug users, while safe spaces were built for people to seek help no matter who they were or how they looked or acted when they showed up. This work is founded out of necessity, to protect people from the threat of the state. QueerCare is a radical collective in London that provides resources for supporting people at risk of state violence, including in mental health detention. If more of us were skilled up to de-escalate situations of crisis, knew how to suture wounds, or had Naloxone on hand to prevent people from overdosing on heroin, fewer of us would end up sectioned, imprisoned and detained.

Comrades in the Kurdish community in Rojava have been developing their own healthcare system, with the aim of reclaiming health from the state and returning it to the people. The system built up slowly with the aim of training doctors and healthcare workers to provide care that is not driven by payment. It prioritises education, empowering people to make informed decisions about their care. The Rojava health assembly comprises a broad range of neighbourhood groups that meet regularly to tackle issues of collective health, such as the quality of housing or environmental conditions, in order to prevent sickness, not respond to it.

In the UK, the Solidarity Apothecary has been helping to sustain thousands of people throughout the pandemic. Nicole Rose is the herbalist behind the project and author of *The*

Prisoner's Herbal, a book about incarcerated people making their own herbal remedies with whatever plants they can get hold of. She is living with chronic illness and health conditions resulting from her imprisonment at the age of nineteen, after a sweep of state repression against animal rights activists. She has supplied tinctures, sprays and other herbal treatments to defendants on trial in the criminal justice system, including to those enduring the ongoing stress of state repression and surveillance as activists and organisers. Her remedies have reached over 4,000 people living in encampments in Calais through her work with Herbalists Without Borders.

'Plants have been accomplices in resistance for thousands of years,' Nicole says. We learn that accounts by enslaved women record the use of plants such as cotton root to induce abortions, in resistance to the use of their bodies to produce more workers for slavers. When we investigate the roots of tiger balm, a soothing, scented balm that people all over the globe rub on their chests, muscles and temples when they're feeling sick, sore or anxious, we discover that it is another ancient remedy created by ancestors in South Asia that people took with them under indentureship to the Caribbean.

Nicole's approach in her one-to-one clinical consultations is very different to the ten-minute doctor's appointments that we typically receive. She takes her time, making sure everything is consensual about her care. She explains the effects of every ingredient and centres the person's needs, not external expectations or unrealistic goals. Nicole's approach and that of other community herbalists is embedded in a history of resistance and struggle, embodying the power of creating ways to take care of our health outside of systems that want us dead.

6.

HOUSING JUSTICE

After Sisters Uncut reclaimed the visitor's centre at Holloway Prison in London in 2017, they took action as part of a local coalition of groups fighting to transform the site of the former prison into safe and affordable housing. Sisters Uncut recognised that for housing to be safe, it must be free of police and state interference and invasion. The proposal by Peabody, the housing association that bought and is developing the HMP Holloway site, is not enough. According to current plans, less than half of the land would be used for flats that are affordable to local residents. The public has also campaigned for the site to house a stand-alone Women's Building, owned by the community, with a wide range of support and facilities for survivors and those impacted by the criminal justice system. Peabody's proposal for a community centre does not fulfil the community's demands; the housing association was able to buy the land with a loan from the Mayor's Office for Police and Crime (MOPAC), and MOPAC services are being considered on the site. The retention of any connection to the criminal justice system would stand in the way of the necessary transformation of the land that formerly housed a violent prison.

Abolition is about building safe communities, which means making sure our homes, streets and neighbourhoods are safe. This requires first and foremost transforming our society's relationship with people experiencing homelessness, treating them with dignity and centring their autonomy, rather than paternalistically deciding what is best for them. In 2015, a group of unknown organisers took action around London at night by covering up anti-homeless architecture to enable people forced onto the streets to sleep safely. People without access to stable housing are vulnerable to violence and abuse. Because of the strong stigma, many of us don't speak openly about our experiences of homelessness, its impacts on our wellbeing and access to employment, and the risks we must sometimes take by living with people who are harmful to us because we have nowhere else to go. Challenging homelessness stigma means that when a homeless person asks for change, we could give them money directly, rather than pretending to suddenly be concerned about drug usage. It would also help to provide sterilised and safe needles for people who are homeless and addicted to substances.

A roof over our heads is not good enough when people are living in conditions that impact their health or where they are vulnerable to violence. Housing activists around Britain are campaigning for tenants' rights and better living conditions. The London Renters Union supports tenants by organising rent strikes and is campaigning for strict rent controls to be placed on private landlords, with swift expropriation of slum landlords who break housing law. A necessary step towards abolition and housing justice is to abolish the landlord–tenant dynamic altogether, with suitable, accessible housing provided for all.

Housing and land that are owned and controlled by the British state, however, will not lead us to the housing justice we need. The state controls a lot of housing in the UK, but it has abused that power on many occasions and neglected vulnerable communities, with tragic impacts. Our friend Milly G. Ali reminds us of Grenfell Tower. 'That's the quality of our houses the state is deciding on, too, how spaces are built, and they're often not what we need.'

Despite legislation passed in 2012 to criminalise squatting residential properties, we can learn a lot from the UK's long history of squatters' resistance, spearheaded by women of colour, migrants, sex workers, queer people and disabled people who were too poor to rent or buy property and had to find alternatives for housing. In the 1970s, it was common to set up squats in empty flats and shops. Olive Morris and Liz Obi squatted in Brixton at 121 Railton Road, which was later turned into a Black radical bookshop called Sabaar. On these premises they hosted countless Black community organising meetings. Another feminist squat near Euston Station provided a space in the 1970s for women from the community to come together and talk about the issues they were facing. Bangladeshi women spoke about being forcibly injected with contraceptives and about the intense racism they were experiencing, and lesbians were able to meet and organise against discrimination. In 1982, the English Collective of Prostitutes, Women Against Rape and Black Women for Wages for Housework occupied a church near Kings Cross in protest of the violent targeting of sex workers by police. A succession of actions and occupations also led to the founding of Crossroads Women's Centre in Kentish Town, now housing around seventeen organisations. Many other women's centres and community spaces all over the country have been hard won by those who desperately need them.

Redistribution of resources is vital for our healing as marginalised communities. 'I feel like for a lot of people, their goal is to someday own their own house or their property,' another friend states. They propose that to build a world without prisons, we must address our own desires to buy property. This could mean working towards communal ownership as a first step. Milly G. Ali shares their family's experience with us: 'When my grandparents moved here decades ago, they didn't have any access to social housing. Loads of families lived together in tiny little terraces, and that made them a target for lots of racism in this country. People still laugh about it now, like, "loads of Asian people stuffed into a house together," but that was their form of survival. I don't agree with the ownership of houses ideologically, but in the context that we live in, people have done that, and it's been life-saving. But I think it's important to transform our housing goals from private ownership to more cooperative living spaces.' As abolitionists, we must expand our imaginations beyond property ownership: our vision requires abolishing not only prisons and the police, but also the private property that necessitates its protection through violent policing.

7.

CARE IN COMMUNITY

When vulnerable young people need support, interventions by the state and the police have the power to cause even more harm. For this reason, Akwaaba, a social centre for migrants in North-East London, is a space that is free of social workers, in order to ensure that no one is exposed to risks of being reported to the Home Office. This is in recognition of the very real threat that seemingly benevolent arms of the state present to people with insecure immigration status.

We need to understand the danger that the state poses to children through the border regime, school exclusions, PREVENT and systemic ableism, pushing young people to the outskirts of society to both experience and cause further harm. If you work within these institutions, what are you doing to challenge the system and redistribute resources into community self-determination? Organisations such as Together with Migrant Children provide examples for how we can begin to create resistance against the harms enacted on children by state neglect and the border regime. We can also support young people to know their rights, advocate for themselves and build community and connection. In 2020, the 4Front Project, a youth-led organising group, founded Jahiem's Justice Centre, a radical youth centre for and by the community in Colindale, London, where most state-run youth services have been closed down.

Understanding that the family can be a place of deep trauma, we need to build networks of support for young people to access the care they might not be receiving at home without ending up in the hands of the state. We also need resources to build safety in our communities, so people don't fear losing their kids because they don't have the financial support they need if they leave their abusive partners. The chosen family is the makeshift, intentional community that queer people have long had to weave for themselves after being rejected by the people who raised them. It enables survival through different forms of communal living and the sharing of childcare and resources.

Speaking to our elders within our communities, we have heard how women have supported each other to leave abusive relationships, keeping each other's most precious items, like photo albums, safe under their beds until their owners are ready to collect them. We have heard how people in our communities have made sure that the childhood sexual abuse they experienced was not repeated with their own children by preventing an abusive grandparent from staying overnight in the same house. We have long kept, and continue to keep, ourselves safer. What we need now is bolder action from everyone to resist violence openly.

Generation Five is a grassroots organisation born in the USA in 2000. It aims to end child sexual abuse within five generations through building community capacity and liberatory approaches to violence that do not rely on the state. Its work focuses on community education about what child abuse is, how to identify patterns of harm, and how to be accountable for and intervene in those cycles. Unlearning our ingrained attitudes of scarcity and punishment is crucial to being able to work towards ending generational abuse, and we can learn so much from the work of Generation Five and from the comprehensive Creative Interventions toolkit.

We need spaces for children and young people to feel safe, to know that they will be believed and heard, however they communicate, and to feel valued and worthy of love and care. Exist Loudly is a grassroots organisation founded by youth worker and activist Tanya Compas that centres care for young queer Black people who have experienced homelessness. It leads by example to show how life is about more than just survival and must involve community and joy.

Woodcraft Folk, a cooperatively run youth movement, puts the values of youth empowerment at the heart of its structure, from having some of the youngest trustees in the country on its board, to organising local groups that follow the lead of children and young people in deciding what to do in their get-togethers. In summer camps and weekly group sessions, children and young people learn about cooperative values through games and practical experience. In 2011, Woodcraft Folk hosted CoCamp, where around 3,000 young people from around the world came together to dream of a sustainable future built on values of interdependency, care and respect. As part of Woodcraft Folk, children of all ages participate in the running of the camps—cooking, cleaning and choosing where to go on a walk are shared activities. It's there that young people learn how to take care of each other and that we share the responsibility of keeping us all safe.

Sometimes, simply having the space to share what we're going through is transformative. Being able to talk about why these things are happening and how they are impacting us, and knowing that other people are impacted too, gives us the opportunity to think about ways we can address our problems. This can lead us to a place of restoration or repair, or it can help us to find a route through the collective pain towards deeper relationships and understandings, giving us lessons to take forward.

Land reparations, housing justice, disability justice and the transformation of our education and healthcare systems are all necessary steps on the way to ending child abuse. It is all interdependent. We must take a holistic approach that recognises that we rely on each other for our safety. We must commit to care by any and all means necessary.

8.

TRANSFORMING EDUCATION

Over the last couple of years, young people across the UK have been campaigning to increase representation of the work, legacy and experiences of people of colour in the school curriculum, so that more students can see themselves reflected in the history and literature they are studying and can reconnect with knowledge that has been hidden by the whitewashing of education. These campaigns touch on an important part of the transformation needed within the education system, but there is much more that has to change in a society that enables the systemic abandonment of children.

Exclusion is often ignored by people who aren't experiencing it, and it is often stigmatised even within the most impacted communities. It's easy to internalise the shame that systems of disposability impose. But many campaigns are being run to raise consciousness of policing and racism in schools and in society, led by powerful youths spotlighting their experiences. One such campaign group is ICFree, which ad-hacked local bus stops in Brixton using posters of young children in the style of police mugshots to highlight the absurdity of criminalising children and to draw the connection between school exclusion and imprisonment. Kids of Colour in Manchester released a detailed report on why police don't belong in schools, sharing experiences and statistics about the traumas inflicted on young people of colour who have been criminalised at school. The group continues to campaign to remove officers from schools around Greater Manchester, encouraging young people in other parts of the country to do the same. No More Exclusions is a national movement with chapters in London, Birmingham and Manchester fighting to abolish school exclusion altogether, lobbying the National Education Union and targeting local councils.

Along with restorative justice practitioner Alex Johnston, Cradle has worked to implement just practices in an independent democratic school in West Norwood, London. The New School's policies do not include typical guidelines for punishment, instead outliningtransformative tools to repair harm within the school community. It's a small, new project, and so far a fruitful experiment, putting into practice ways to approach conflict as a communal issue, rather than an individual one that results in the isolation and abandonment of a child. More schools must be willing to try something different.

Writer, rapper and public educator Akala has spoken publicly about the important role of his community's pan-African Saturday school in teaching him about Black history, a topic totally absent from his full-time schooling. It's not just that the books read in British schools are written by white people. It's that the entire understanding of how the world works is imparted through the lens of and for the benefit of white supremacy. Isaac Newton, for example, developed his theory of gravity using measurements of ocean tides in different locations, some of which he had access to because of the international slave trade, notably the French slave ports in Martinique. When so much of our understanding of the world is steeped in white supremacy, the focus remains on testing, competition and class status. But education is a lifelong process that should be aimed not toward creating productive and obedient workers, but rather toward inspiring confident, kind and creative members of society.

A transformative learning space would focus on growth and community building. It would value the wisdom of both youth and ancestry. It would expand our knowledge by engaging with perspectives expressed within language and culture nearly lost to colonialism. It would break down binaries of teacher and student, integrating learning more deeply into our communities to dismantle intergenerational barriers as well as the barriers between disciplines. It would change the whole shape of our education system. What are the things we learn about the land in a science lab that we could learn in a garden growing food for our families?

We must commit—together—to learning what it is to be in community with each other and to giving space for young people to pursue knowledge in order to build power toward change.

9.

THE END OF CAPITALISM

'For every nickel I get, the company makes a dime
That's why I organise on company time'
—Trade unionist chant

Wages and benefits will not keep pace with the rising cost of living without our demanding it. Individual success under capitalism won't free us. Working people have to rise up together, but so do the middle classes, because we are all being exploited by the super-wealthy 1%. To dismantle this system, we must critically examine the economic, political and social factors that have allowed our exploitation as workers and the exploitation of communities around the world. Resources must be redistributed and reparations made.

Socialism is a political-economic structure that disrupts existing class hierarchies and aims to create social equality, where resources are communally owned and all people have access to housing, universal basic income, free healthcare and free education. This is a radical shift from the logic of capitalism, which concentrates ownership and wealth in the hands of a few, generating massive disparities in the distribution of resources and opportunities and valuing profits over people.

Abolition is born of the legacy of revolts by those forced to labour under transatlantic slavery; the Haitian Revolution forged a path for so many Black liberation movements to come. Solidarity among people whose labour is exploited is thus at the very heart of the struggle for liberation from capitalism and is key to realising the vision of an abolitionist world. In today's context in Britain, working-class struggles against exploitation are led mainly by workers within unions. Although unions are not the only vehicle for worker solidarity, they have a long and radical history in this country. By building collective power to stand up to capital, unions can provide a vital service towards eliminating insecure, poorly paid, highly alienated and labour-intensive work for everyone.

Workers under capitalism have always had to band together to advocate for themselves. If you work to live, you are a worker. We have common interests: get paid more, improve conditions at work, get more holiday time and breaks, and get timely responses to our grievances. Despite our common interests, collective action is undermined by the individualist incentive to benefit from the radical actions of others without contributing. So called 'freeriding' makes labour organisation more difficult by giving temporary benefits to individual workers who avoid unions or break strikes. In response, workers and unions must provide stronger incentives to organise, including striking the right balance between closed unions with compulsory membership and open unions with voluntary membership.

Worker solidarity means centring the most marginalised workers in society, the Black, brown and migrant workers who are in the lowest-paid and most precarious jobs, as capitalism is a system built on racism. Solidarity entails listening to the demands of Amazon workers and Deliveroo workers in the gig economy when they ask us to participate in strikes and boycotts. It also means supporting initiatives like the SOAS Justice for Cleaners campaign, which emerged in 2006 and has since spread to universities across London. These groups are led by university cleaning staff who organise for better pay and working conditions, as they are often subcontracted with no access to university benefits and have been forced to work with no hazard pay or protective gear during the pandemic.

Within unionising also lies one avenue towards the necessary disentanglement of people's jobs from the prison industrial complex. Unions for workers in the charity and care work sectors should help people in the fight against PREVENT and against mandatory reporting laws that turn support systems into tentacles of policing and border control. Construction worker unions could organise in companies taking on new prison projects in a powerful move towards liberation. We must resist being forced to build our own cages.

We are not experts in economics and are not seeking to propose to our readers an entire alternative economic structure. Other groups such as Decolonising Economics are making strides in bringing this important knowledge to marginalised communities so we can begin the work of dismantling capitalism, a system that fuels white European violence against the earth and the human communities of the world. As abolitionists, we must hold in mind our ultimate goal of reducing all types of harm: opportunistic and professional, interpersonal and institutional, military and environmental, financial and political.

Cradle recognises the exploitation we all experience under white-supremacist, patriarchal capitalism, as well as what Claudia Jones described as the superexploitation of Black women under these systems. We believe the remedies to these are decolonisation, redistribution and building societies centred on mutual aid where everyone has the means to thrive. In a world where we didn't have to commit most of our energy to making enough money to keep a roof over our heads, we might actually have time to engage in the self-reflection, community care and collective healing work that will truly sustain us.

10.

DISABILITY JUSTICE

Covid-19 is a mass disabling event that has highlighted the extent to which 'health' is a privilege. Something as simple as catching a virus or having an infection can lead you to be disabled for the rest of your life. 'People are getting this wake-up call now that it's easy to become disabled,' says our friend Eshe. 'A lot of people thought, well, if we were disabled, we would do it differently, we would work through the whole thing, we would go to the doctors, we would be fine. Now they're realising we weren't just saying all of this shit about how being disabled is so difficult, that actually this is the reality, and their jobs discard them, the government discards them, the NHS discards them so quickly when it becomes a long-term health problem and not a short-term health problem.'

So much of society is inaccessible to many of us, but it doesn't have to be this way. When the coronavirus pandemic forced the world online, universities and workplaces suddenly figured out how to operate in accessible ways, revealing what disabled people have always known: that ableism is a choice. Moreover, as many disabled people have noted, lots of people continue to be excluded despite some recent improvements in accessibility, such as in Covid-safe outdoor dining spaces with restricted wheelchair access.

The problem of disability lies in society, not in the bodies of disabled people. Rather than asking disabled people what made them disabled, we need to question the ableist conditions that can make disability into a crime. How we conceptualise disability shifts according to societal conditions. Many people who wear glasses would not consider themselves disabled, but if access to glasses were as limited as wheelchair ramps, poor eyesight would transform from a naturally occurring human trait into a disability. Much like criminality, disability is constructed, and just like with criminality, harm and violence can lead to disability. Oppressive conditions in society can also make people disabled, like being forced to work during a life-threatening pandemic, or living in unsafe homes that cause health problems. This was the case for Ella Adoo-Kissi-Debrah, a nine-year-old Black girl from Lewisham, who died in 2013 from asthma made worse by air pollution in her area. We need to ask who has access to health and what it means to be healthy under a system in which doctors regularly deny the bodily autonomy of fat people, and migrants have limited recourse to a health service that collaborates with the Home Office and the police.

Of course, we are not suggesting that in an abolitionist future, no one would be disabled. The pain that people experience needs to be acknowledged, and the challenges of neurodiversity cannot solely be attributed to living under capitalism. Our message is that illness should not be criminalised or a barrier to fully participating in society, and that our notions of disability and normality are determined by an oppressive system. We must also recognise that ableism impacts everyone, and so does accessibility. For example, during the Covid pandemic, the sudden ability to access events taking place online across the world was beneficial to all of us.

Thanks to the work of Sins Invalid, Mia Mingus and Talia Lewis, we know that abolition will only be made possible through disability justice. Disability justice is body-neutral and values everyone regardless of how productive we are; our collective liberation will be achieved by all of us together. Disabled people have always done the work of practising freedom and collaborating with each other through peer support and mutual aid, and we have so much to learn from this history. It is because of disabled people, who have always found alternative ways of tending to our bodies and surviving this ableist world, that we were able to adapt to our new Covid reality. Disability justice takes an intersectional approach and values the expertise of those who intimately understand the multiple ways that our current system weaves harm and violence into our lives—disabled sex workers, disabled people of colour and disabled people held within carceral institutions.

One of the principles of transformative justice is interdependence, the importance of which we can learn from disability justice activists. We all have access needs, whether that be medication to help us concentrate or contact lenses to help us see. Interdependence rather than independence challenges the idea of disabled people as a burden. We do not live isolated lives in our communities, but the state uses inaccessibility as a tool to breed isolation. To challenge this and support each other, we can no longer consider accessibility as an after-thought; it is not enough to have a wheelchair ramp for an event if there is no sign-language interpreter present. Disabled people have a wide range of accessibility needs, and in order to meet them, we need to listen to disabled people.

Eshe refers to the project of building 'full-spectrum community care', a system designed to support the needs of the most marginalised people, rather than prioritising those of the most privileged. Disability justice also requires us to centre the autonomy of disabled people, who know their bodies better than any doctor ever can. We need to focus on and believe people describing their pain and their problems. We could throw theory at it and say that in an abolitionist world, this wouldn't happen, but it is happening. We have to be able to support people right now. If our chronically ill friend is being gaslighted by doctors, we can offer to attend an appointment to act as an advocate. When a friend is having a flare-up of illness, we can help them with their tasks. We can help our comrades to fill out the lengthy and violent forms that the state requires of them to access disability benefits. This is disability justice.

As long as capitalism stands, we will continue to see more and more people with chronic illness and health problems caused by burnout and state violence. Therefore, we need to figure out ways of healing together in order to heal society, and that starts with the most vulnerable. In order for us to survive capitalism and live long enough to inhabit the new world we are building, we must learn from disabled people who remind us to rest and slow down and be patient with our bodies and minds.

11.

HEALTHY MINDS

We all have the capacity to suffer from a crisis of mental illness, and most people will experience fluctuations in their mental health throughout their life. When this happens, even in our own lives, we can see that the responses of Western psychiatry are often shaped by racism and patriarchy, which are embedded into its ideology and practices. This is not to say that psychiatric care has not helped many individuals to cope with the hardships of life under capitalism, but rather that in spite of this, we cannot ignore psychiatry's carceral functions and its role in the growth of the prison industrial complex. Psychiatry has long served to label certain people as disordered and untreatable, and this in turn has rendered some groups politically and socially invisible. Moreover, our current mental health system removes madness from its political context of poor housing, precarity and isolation. While mental health treatment may have shifted on the surface since the notorious days of the asylum, our conceptions of health continue to align with the same logics that permit incarceration and state violence, focusing on reactive care rather than holistic, preventative approaches.

The situation is so dire that many of us expend most of our energy simply trying to survive the traumatic and oppressive conditions of society that drive us mad. Our communities deserve more. We can't continue to call for funding for mental health services that punish and control us, rationing care according to white-supremacist ideas about who is deserving and who is disposable. To fully thrive, we need to be able to conceptualise healthy minds beyond our functionality as workers under capitalism. Our need for medication and therapy would not magically disappear but would drastically change if we were to alleviate the pressures of exploitative employment, extortionate rent and precarious housing.

The abolition of the mental health industrial complex requires us to reimagine safety outside of carceral systems, where mental health diagnoses are not tools of criminalisation but sites of support for each other. By centring a politics of care, we can build a culture that is anti-violence and pro-consent, where we maintain our autonomy, treat each other with compassion and find ways to support our collective healing. We must ensure that every person is safe to live freely, understanding that individual suffering cannot be separated from the health of our community. We have a responsibility towards each other. Abuse, fear and loneliness are all impacts of society's responses to those who are mentally vulnerable. If trauma can be passed through the body through generations, we need to cultivate the world of care that our descendants will inherit.

This requires us to depathologise and decriminalise the range of human emotions and behaviours that we are taught to demonise. Instead of calling the police when someone is having a mental health crisis, we should centre the autonomy of the person who is in distress by building more creative options to respond. While we may not know exactly what to do, we do know how to treat someone with humanity. When witnessing a crisis, we can ask a person what they need and think about what we would need in their situation, and we can build our skills in de-escalation. With our loved ones, we can discuss which tools work best to support them during a crisis. No one knows our own mind better than we do.

We don't need professionals to dictate care for our communities. It is time to champion peer support and stop relying on systems that don't care about us to help us in the moments where we most need care. Groups like QueerCare and the US-based group Project LETS show us that it is possible to hold space for vulnerability and protect each other based on disability justice models of interdependence and mutual aid. In a hyper-individualistic society that labels certain people as disposable, nurturing and treating people with love and kindness if they are sick is transformative justice work.

Care work has historically been treated as unworthy of pay and attention. But in the face of unrelenting violence, resistance through community care will make this society that works us to the bone obsolete.

12.

TRANS LIBERATION

> *'What will the world look like after the abolition of gender? I don't know, is my answer. And I think that's okay. Just as long as it's not this. The whole point is that it's meant to be about a new world, new futures, imagination. So anything I say will pale in comparison to what could be, because we haven't lived anything else. We haven't known anything else. And we haven't tried yet. So I don't know. And I'm okay with that.'*
>
> — Fopé Ajanaku

Trans liberation represents a natural path to abolition through the rejection of the binaristic violence of a transphobic society. In this sense, to be queer is to be against the state. Trans people are born into a world that actively works to regulate and punish their being, which means the trans experience is frequently marked by pain and suffering. Trans liberation is a movement to recentre the joy and communalism inherent in queer life. We could learn from the ways that trans people, in particular trans people of colour, have always lived collectively with an understanding that 'we keep us safe'.

'Protect Black trans women' is an empty statement when their GoFundMes fail to reach their targets and working-class trans people of colour are left passing around the same £10 between themselves to help each other survive. Groups like UK Mutual Aid provide essential platforms for white cis people to donate to trans people of colour. Supporting trans liberation means helping trans people to be able to fund their life-affirming surgery without needing to jump through the NHS's restrictive hoops. It means helping trans people off the street, through shelters like the Outside Project in London. It is time to materially support the most marginalised amongst us.

'To abolish gender roles, you have to abolish prisons and you have to abolish the state as the prime enforcers of these roles,' states our friend Sami. With this understanding in mind, Cradle rejects carceral liberal measures offered to trans people by the state, such as a proposal by the Scottish government to build a prison for non-binary people. We want no trans people in prison. Instead, we champion the work of trans-led abolitionist groups, like Trans Survival, Trans Defence, which provides community support to trans people in prison through letter-writing and inside–outside organising.

Currently, many trans rights campaigns centre on gaining state recognition for trans identity, such as markers on passports for non-binary people. In the words of artist and activist Jacob V. Joyce, 'I don't want a gender that's recognised by the state—that would obviously be a neoliberal tactic. This state could never recognise my gender, because it's built on white-supremacist, capitalist, heteropatriarchal land exploitation and body exploitation. How could that ever recognise me as a full human being?'

As abolitionists, we are careful to consider whether our actions will legitimise the state through encouraging reforms. Sami asks, 'Is this a reform that we are going to have to undo later? You start talking about third-gender categorisation systems on passports—aside from the fact that I don't want it in general, I don't want to be on some kind of state register for trans people. That sounds like a nightmare.' Strengthening the tools of the carceral state will only ever harm trans people when the law is inherently violent and transphobic. This means we must reject hate crime legislation as a solution to transphobic and queerphobic violence. We are not going to abolish transphobia by turning to the state for legitimacy or protection.

What purposes does the gender binary serve and what does it disallow? Trans liberation means gender self-determination, the freedom to define, change or reject our gender in its entirety, and abolition provides this possibility for us all—to be transformed as we co-create new ways of existing. Gender self-determination should not depend on surviving long enough to reach adulthood, or on proving to a panel of cis people that you have adequately lived 'in role' according to society's gender norms. The state does not get to determine who is allowed to be trans based on the false notion that transness is harmful to the world. We are no longer accepting conditions on our liberation.

There are so many ways in which we are taught to maintain and regulate our bodies, but bodily autonomy is a necessary condition for freedom. Our bodies are our own. We have to abolish the pathologisation of trans people and the medical gatekeeping to surgical transition. One aspect of building trans liberation could mean the community production of hormones like oestrogen or testosterone. This could be similar to the work of the Catalonia-based collective GynePunk, who are finding ways to conduct smear tests at home in order to take power away from the medical industry and instead create systems of healthcare that centre patient autonomy.

As Sami says, 'People should be able to transition, detransition, retransition as many times as they like, and that should be funded freely ... You should be able to experiment with your body or swap into bodies, finding ways of seizing the means of gender production.'

13.

ABOLITION FEMINISM

Abolition feminism asks us to build communities that respond proactively to sexual violence and to put the needs of survivors at the centre of our responses. Police need to be abolished from the lives of survivors as a matter of urgency. We seek to end gender-based violence once and for all.

'I firmly believe that there's nothing that can be done after the fact that properly remedies bodily invasion,' says Lola Olufemi. 'The body is so fundamental to how we think, move and exist in the world. Even if some survivors say it gave them peace of mind when their abuser was in prison, so many will say that this experience has impacted their entire life, changed everything about the way that they relate to other people. There has to be a way of thinking that recognises that the aim is not to rectify harm, because rectifying that specific kind of harm is impossible. When you recognise that to be read as a woman, or to be read in a way that's anything other than a man, opens you up to so much violence that you have to dodge and skip around as you grow older, how can prison put an end to that? Abolition makes us think about how we might be able to craft systems that stop that violence from happening in the first place.'

Experiences of sexual violence are the cause of deep pain for survivors. Whether it be harassment by a stranger on the street or being raped by someone you trust, this violence is serious, and we are committed to taking it seriously. We don't see a route to safety through a system that has exported sexual violence all over the world. Instead, abolition feminism gives us a frame to look through to a world without coercion, violence and domination.

To end sexual violence in our communities, we first need to take responsibility for the cultures in which we participate. We must practise our skills in intervening in misogyny in any form, whether that's calling out a colleague for a sexist joke, or pulling a friend aside for a chat when we notice them shaming their partner's outfit on a night out. We need to recognise that there is no single image of what a 'rapist' looks like, and that these myths protect people who cause harm from being accountable. We need to build systems of accountability where members of the community can feel equipped to step in and address violence, both by supporting the survivor to figure out and meet their needs, and by holding space for the person who caused harm to learn to do better and respect boundaries that are put in place. Not everyone wants the same things, and we need to create systems that have the necessary flexibility to hold different ways that people respond to trauma. We must aim not to react to harm with more harm.

To cut sexual violence out of our lives at its source, we have to end patriarchy and all forms of systemic domination. To do this, we must demolish constructed, dehumanising hierarchies of gender, race, sexuality and disability. We must raise our children with agency over their own bodies and with respect for those of others. We must dismantle the colonial, capitalist structures that enable exploitation and extraction not just of our resources but also of our bodies, by fighting against borders and imperialist intervention. We must resist all state powers that allow police and prison officers to violate those in their custody. We must intervene in the abusive dynamics that exist in society to silence survivors and those around them through the threat of losing jobs, homes and families. We must take action collectively in our communities to name violence and cut it off before it can take root.

Transformative justice asks us to try to change the conditions of power imbalance and control that embed abuse and violence in our cultures. It is an approach that prioritises supporting marginalised people and survivors, stopping harm from happening right now, and developing systems for reflection and accountability. It helps us to begin rebuilding safer communities grounded in care, solidarity and mutual aid and gives us hope that we can prevent violence from continuing to be repeated over generations.

Consent culture is fundamentally threatened by coercion and exploitation under capitalism, and many survivors will be silenced until we dismantle the oppressive structures described in the previous chapters. But as we build a safer society, radically transforming our approaches to health, education, housing and care, abolitionist feminists also work hard to look after each other and help each other to cope with their own experiences of trauma and violence.

Crossroads Women's Centre in Kentish Town, London acts as a support base for women from marginalised communities, including sex workers and people impacted by detention and imprisonment. Centres like these were founded by women from a range of backgrounds, and many of their organisers were aligned with the internationalist and anti-imperialist Black liberation movements of the 1970s and '80s. As so many revolutionaries in those years travelled between nations to meet and strategise with each other, the history and influence of these spaces transcends borders. Andaiye, a revolutionary from Guyana and founding member of the Working People's Alliance, visited London to make connections with activists there and was present for some of the occupations that led to the creation of Crossroads in Kentish Town. She was later involved in setting up a women's centre, which shares the name Crossroads, in Guyana to house a feminist organisation called

Red Thread. This legacy of feminist internationalism shows the power of revolutionary solidarity and the interconnectedness of our struggles to end all forms of violence.

While the ins and outs of Britain's rape culture are specific, sexual violence and patriarchy are prevalent across the globe. Many of the organisers of the Global Women's Strike, who fought internationally for unpaid feminised labour to be recognised and valued, were deeply entrenched in anti-violence work too. Their activism shows an understanding of how domestic labour, reproductive rights and sexual violence are all issues of agency over the bodies of women and gender-non-conforming people, rooted in the restrictions created by poverty in a patriarchal society.

Sisters Uncut is a feminist direct action group founded in 2014 in response to the deadly impacts of austerity on domestic violence services that people rely on for survival. Its organising focus has since moved from austerity towards abolition, and its work takes place within a growing movement of abolitionist feminists in the UK resisting carceral responses to violence. Sisters Uncut follows the feminist legacy of direct action, such as when the group's North London chapter set its sights on the reclamation of the recently emptied site of Holloway Prison. As part of Reclaim Holloway, a coalition of local housing, anti-gentrification and feminist groups, Sisters Uncut organised to resist moves by the council to sell the land to developers for the construction of luxury flats. The coalition demanded social housing and a community building dedicated to supporting women and gender-non-conforming people. In May 2017, Sisters Uncut took action and broke into the empty visitors' centre on the prison site in a historic political occupation. The group temporarily transformed the dingy, dirty space to hold a community festival for women and gender-non-conforming people and children to share meals and wisdom. They remained there for a week, holding workshops, meetings and activities. The occupation was a bold experiment in finding out how to take responsibility for a space and for your people, to build your own community of care.

Reclaiming space, in our experience at least, has been necessary in realising a new vision for our world, enabling us to create desperately needed support systems that do not mimic the dynamics of abusers, to feel safe with each other and to build trust and solidarity. An abolitionist feminist revolution could be a wave of occupations across the globe in which the people take back space and housing for oppressed communities. Imagine community spaces where survivors of domestic and state violence could go at any time to chat, eat and soothe their anxieties with people who understand and who won't get them deported or arrested. This should not be difficult to picture; in fact, we create these spaces in small ways all the time whenever we validate the pain of our friends or step in when we see someone being harassed on the street. As Ivié Itoje shares from her experience working in the women's sector, many mutual support principles are already in practice, despite state repression. 'So many of the women that we serve in the community let other migrant women use their bank accounts, which then messes up their application [for state support]. People let other people use their ID cards, or let people stay in their council flat—which you would literally get thrown in prison for if social services find out—or these other ways of not having to include the state in what's happening. It's in practice already.' It is important for us to fight for each other's survival in these covert ways and challenge the punishments handed out in response, while also eliminating the root causes of violence and building an abolitionist future.

Violence doesn't have to be normal. As well as nurturing ways to protect and support each other to heal from harm, we must also abolish the structures that produce and perpetuate it in the first place. The criminal justice system is wielded by an abusive state to reinforce rape culture, scapegoating certain figures who represent violence in the popular imagination, and letting other violence enacted by the powerful go unpunished. Building a feminist future requires us to dismantle all institutions that hinder our liberation and to remake our world around safety, collective action, accountability and transformation.

14.

OUR STORIES

'Imagining and telling lies are not the same'
—Jemma Desai

Writers who create police officer characters for TV are not impartial and are unlikely to have experienced criminalisation. Even in shows that highlight some aspects of police corruption or brutality, the violence of the criminal justice system is usually depicted as the result of a few 'bad apples'. And when imagining an alternative world without police, TV writers seem limited to recycling just a handful of options: stories based on a desert island (a colonial trope), in the afterlife, in a post-apocalyptic future, or in outer space (although mainstream sci-fi does tend to involve a lot of space cops). What would happen if, instead, stories were told about collective care and survivor-centred justice? How could the entertainment industry be built around collaboration and solidarity instead of hierarchy and exploitation?

Taking on these problems with the intention of opening space for new stories is Means TV: the first worker-owned and openly anti-capitalist streaming service. Means operates on a subscription service, like Netflix, platforming only original content and creating new shows and films that tell worker-led stories. It was created as a direct response to the issues presented by capitalist mainstream media.

Fictional heroes in films and TV shows reinforce the idea that we must outsource issues in our communities to strong higher powers. 'I think taking the law into your own hands as an individual is very often seen as a really bad thing that you shouldn't ever do,' says one TV writer. 'But Luther [a detective] can knock down doors, right?' Instead of portraying the public as powerless and in need of saviours, we could 'tell stories that show community cohesion and communities working together, in a way that allows people to see what that looks like. These stories exist, they're just not being told.'

Some imaginative TV storylines have shown us glimpses of the support and justice we crave. In the BBC series *I May Destroy You*, the storytellers make space for a sexual violence survivor to work out what justice and healing could look like in many different iterations; she ultimately arrives at solution that is independent of an ongoing police investigation. In the Netflix original *Sex Education*, a young person is traumatised after being sexually assaulted on the bus and is beautifully supported by her friends in a simple but meaningful way when they commit to accompanying her on the way to school until she feels safe to be alone. Across television genres, there have been many subtle and impactful moments depicting queer joy, vulnerability between partners and compassionate parenting. But these stories are still rare amid a steady stream of copaganda; moreover, they are still being produced and sold within an industry constructed to maintain the lifestyle and power of billionaires.

Since connecting with producers for this chapter, some members of Cradle Community accepted an invitation to attempt to sow seeds of accountability across the entertainment industry after decades of cyclical abuse. Several years after the #MeToo movement drew attention to widespread sexual abuse and harassment, little has changed—though apparently

Netflix put out some guidelines restricting eye contact between colleagues to less than five seconds. Cradle is now involved in building community care into the production of a new television series, with the aim of encouraging people to take on the responsibility to disrupt violence and dismantle the mechanisms that silence survivors. The impact of this work is hugely constricted by the massive pay disparities in place in the industry and by the overarching power of the companies that commission programmes, so it is vital for us to collaborate with those fighting for better workers' rights across the production. By starting conversations about how we take responsibility for our actions and for each other's wellbeing in the entertainment workplace, we can start to transform the dynamics and priorities behind the camera in order to build something new in front of it.

Fighting for our stories might mean pushing against the constraints of what can be written for mainstream broadcasters, or unionising in and disrupting existing spaces. It could be crowdfunding to produce your own pilot, or creating content for social media even knowing that it could be blocked by algorithms or deleted. It could be supporting and building alternative media platforms like Means. If you are a filmmaker or screenwriter, we urge you to think deeply before putting police in your story. Ask what purpose they are serving, and what narratives the characters are reinforcing or resisting. Reflect on the ways that 'diversity' is being used, remembering that marginalised people are worth more than our trauma.

Television is a hugely powerful force in our culture, and it is being used very strategically by the powerful to shape narratives about our world. But across our many connected struggles, it is possible to counter those narratives. We can build new structures—by collectives to serve collectives—reclaiming the power to tell our own stories. This way, we can experiment with what we are building and envision a world in which we thrive.

4.

FREE THEM ALL

To build an abolitionist future, we must commit to the idea that nobody, no matter their crime, deserves to be dehumanised and violated, and that control and surveillance do not enable us to build trust or repair relationships. Contrary to popular opinion, we reckon the doors to all the prisons could fling open tomorrow and the majority of us would be in no more personal danger than before. We acknowledge, however, the context we live in and the unlikelihood of immediate mass release. We argue that this is the result of the state's need for prisons to maintain power, facilitated by the media's fear-mongering about people in prisons, more than it is to prevent a wild surge in violence, a prospect often used to dismiss abolition and to argue for reform.

Our work is to strategically stem the flow of state violence while building what we need to get our people free, through decarceration and mutual aid.

1.

NO MORE PRISONS

The prison industrial complex is growing. In 2019, the Ministry of Justice planned to increase the number of cages, under many new names, to imprison 10,000 more people by 2023. This is part of the British government's longstanding tendency to respond to poverty, mental health struggles and even public health with more police on our streets and more prisons, detention centres and other forms of state custody. We must resist the current plans to build new women's prisons and 'secure schools'; the first of these children's prisons is planned to open in Medway, Kent. In Scotland, the government has proposed to build a mega-prison outside of Glasgow and some small women's units in deprived Glasgow suburbs. The immigration detention centre Morton Hall was closed down but will be reopened as a prison for 'foreign nationals'; we expect this to be a trend that continues. To abolish prisons and policing, first we have to stop their growth.

The Crown Prosecution Service justifies building more prisons by pointing to prison overcrowding and the public's fear of crime—the reality of which is not impacted by building more prisons. The expansion of the prison system cannot be accepted on the grounds that current prisons have been allowed to become overcrowded and to fall into disrepair. HMP Barlinnie in Scotland, for example, is overcrowded and deemed 'unfit for purpose', and so it is being used to justify the construction of mega-prison HMP Glasgow. What about the people who are left exposed to the inhumane conditions of their cells right now? And in the time that it takes to build a prison, couldn't overcrowding be prevented by releasing more people? It is also important to point out that while new prisons are being built, the slowing or even brief decrease in numbers of people entering prisons can be deceptive; with the rise in use of electronic monitoring tags, curfews, community sentences and mandatory treatment, more people are under state control than ever. And as soon as these new institutions start to be opened, the police will find people to fill them.

A war of attrition is underway. Organisers are grinding down and blockading, at times literally, the continuous expansion of surveillance and state control in our lives. The state's appetite for imprisonment and punishment is insatiable, but its eyes are bigger than its stomach. It has forged ahead with plans to construct mega-prisons across England and Scotland even as contracted companies struggle to stay afloat to complete the projects, such as Interserve, which pulled out of the Glen Parva development, and Kier, which has been financially precarious for some time. In a £1 billion deal in 2021, four companies—ISG, Kier, Laing O'Rourke and Wates—were appointed to build four new prisons. Construction has also continued throughout the Covid-19 pandemic, prioritising prisons over the safety of construction workers who have been forced to work in dangerous conditions without adequate personal protective equipment.

What a transparent and exploitative choice it is to build prisons in parts of the country where people have lost jobs and experienced the worst long-term impacts of de-industrialisation and austerity, such as the Midlands, the North West and the South East. After an old prison was shutdown in Wellingborough, some of the town's local residents expressed a desire for a new one, since access to other jobs is scarce in the area. This is not an unusual stance—yet campaigners in South Wales were able to resist and ultimately defeat proposed plans for a mega-prison in Port Talbot, rejecting the presumption that jobs in prisons would be beneficial for the community more widely. Campaigners understood that more labour would be exploited within the new prison than employment would be provided for the local community.

Fight Toxic Prisons and the Prison Ecology Project are abolitionist campaigns that defeated a proposal to build what would have been the largest federal prison in US history in Kentucky (occupied Shawnee, Cherokee, Chickasaw and Osage land). We have learned from their broad yet strategic organising approach how effective it can be to build relationships across unexpectedly aligned groups that are impacted when a new prison is proposed for construction. Strong coalitions with environmental campaigners, legal experts, local residents, unions, anarchists, anti-gentrification and land justice organisers, local politicians and inside campaigners can collectively build resistance to every stage in the process of building a prison. Activist actions often aim to draw out the process and create obstacles to construction; often, if a project takes a lot longer than initially planned, it risks running out of money.

Organisers have been getting creative in how they put pressure on companies to pull out of prison building contracts. Petitions, phone zaps and direct action have been very effective ways to disrupt the process of prison expansion. Delays caused by a single blockade by fewer than ten people at the entrance to the construction site of a new prison at Wellingborough reportedly cost contractor Kier an additional £1.5 million. Actions work, and by organising together to halt prison building and to make it an undesirable industry, we can stop the expansion of the prison industrial complex.

2.

ABOLITIONIST STEPS

As abolitionists, we are not trying to reform or 'fix' prisons or policing. One of our primary aims is to dedicate our energy to work that gets more of our people out of prison, not that leads more of us inside. The more complex and embedded the criminal justice system becomes in our lives, the more difficult it is to divest from and dismantle it.

It is easy to say that it is not realistic to envision a world without prisons, but we learn from and embrace the abolitionists who have provided a blueprint for liberation through direct action and decarceration strategies. This includes the urgent work of the Sex Worker Advocacy and Resistance Movement (SWARM) and Release, which are campaigning for the decriminalisation of sex work and drugs respectively. When Covid-19 struck, abolitionist groups like Community Action on Prison Expansion (CAPE) launched campaigns demanding the release of every single person in prison. These campaigns build a counternarrative to reformist ideas about 'low- and high-risk prisoners', which tell us more about a person's race than their ability to survive in society outside of prison. Building resistance against prisons means freeing them all.

In the previous chapters, we have highlighted the integration of carcerality and punishment into all areas of our lives and outlined many steps towards a holistic vision of abolition. Here we offer some measures that relate specifically to the abolition of policing and prisons, prioritising the defunding of police and challenging the notion that the criminal justice system supports public safety. Abolitionists across the UK worked together to come up with this list of goals and demands.

- Stop the construction of new prisons and of prisons under new names.
- Divest from and target international corporations profiting from securitisation and settler colonialism.
- Demand that our institutions divest from these violently parasitic corporations.
- End the police's use of lethal weapons and other cruel tools, such as firearms, tasers and spit hoods. Redirect funds from police equipment, vehicles and weapons into community-empowering resources.
- Abolish stop and search—one of the key tactics used to harass and criminalise young people of colour. Organisations such as Y-Stop provide tools and apps to help log stop-and-search incidents.
- Abolish PREVENT and the Gangs Matrix. Resist conspiring with these kinds of racist frameworks in whatever spaces they show up.
- Decriminalise sex work.
- Repeal laws that criminalise survival, e.g. drug laws and vagrancy laws, and release everyone imprisoned for those offences.
- Establish confidentiality between services and the people they support. Abolish mandatory reporting.
- Resist new bills to expand policing and probation powers. The Kill the Bill coalition of feminist groups and groups fighting against police brutality, for protest rights, for migrants' rights, against the criminalisation of GRT communities and against child imprisonment have all joined together in resistance to the Police,

Crime, Sentencing and Courts Bill, bringing hundreds of thousands out onto the streets on 1 May 2021.

- Establish community defence against state intervention.
- Spread information about your rights and resources to support people experiencing criminalisation in your local area. Local police monitoring projects are already set up in London, Manchester and other cities across the UK and are an important tool for keeping track of police actions in our communities.

3.

INSIDE–OUTSIDE ORGANISING FOR FREEDOM

Abolition is not about ignoring people who are incarcerated. The movement was born out of the experiences and demands of people locked up in prisons, detention centres and mental health institutions, as well as those of the communities that are directly and indirectly impacted by systems of punishment and incarceration. Families, friends and organisers who fight for abolition have always maintained close relationships with people inside to support them through the daily horrors of prison life. Abolitionists have drafted countless emails, connected people to lawyers, driven across the country to scream outside prison walls, and taken whatever action possible to build pressure on individual prisons to provide medical treatment and basic necessities, often doing so more effectively than the charities whose supposed job is to support our loved ones in prison.

Prisons severely repress those voices inside the walls that are speaking out against the system in any way. Phone calls and post are closely monitored, with a risk of brutal retaliation by guards and parole boards in the form of physical torture or bureaucracy amounting to psychological torture. This can include the denial of access to basic facilities and needs, such as showers, exercise and phone calls, or delays in parole hearings and in transfers to different prisons. Building coordinated resistance is challenging and ongoing work.

Autonomous support groups for people in prison are nothing new in the UK. Families of incarcerated people in campaigns like Smash IPP and Joint Enterprise Not Guilty by Association have been fighting the cases of their loved ones every day for many years. Anarchists and abolitionists have been working to spotlight specific cases of violent treatment and medical neglect experienced by people inside on social media, and to build pressure from the outside by flooding the phone lines of prison governors with concerned callers. Prisons rely on people inside being isolated and stigmatised by the outside world. In conjunction with inside resistance, knowing that the community outside is aware of what's going on inside has been an effective catalyst for change in many cases where people have been denied medications or other necessities.

Groups such as the Parolee Support Network, the Prisoner Solidarity Network and UK Mutual Aid are focusing on decarceration—freeing our people. Combining various methods, they try to increase the chances of people being paroled, particularly IPP prisoners, who face an unfeasible number of bureaucratic barriers to release, often including attendance of behavioural courses that are not available in their prisons. Together, these organisations build networks of support and community to try to prevent people from being recalled. Connected by solicitors who have clients coming up for parole, members write letters and begin to build relationships with people inside, helping them to work out what they might need if they are released. They assist in putting in place what is necessary to tick certain boxes for the parole board's criteria and help people coming out of prison to find housing, community and support with their experiences of state violence.

As far as we know, we are yet to ignite a nationwide prison labour strike in England, Wales or Scotland. But as abolitionist groups continue to build solidarity with more than just the odd isolated individual inside, outside support is beginning to embolden our comrades in prison, at least by letting them know that there are people who can draw attention to the retribution they face when they resist.

5.

TRANSFORMING OUR WORLD

While a liberal lens makes us think that to change the world we only have to change ourselves, as revolutionaries we know we have to change everything. But that doesn't let us off the hook. Even within a transformed world, harm, violence and abuse can still take place. There is still vital work that must be done for us to be in community with each other and to heal from centuries of oppression. This is the vision-building work of transformative justice, which asks us to dismantle the conditions that lead to harm so that it cannot happen again.

It is important that transformative justice does not become a buzzword to be co-opted by the state, in the way that many prisons across Britain implement so-called restorative justice practices. Our transformative work must remain in our own hands in order to keep us safe as intended. The state is constantly evolving and transforming, finding new modes of violence, and therefore our work must do the same.

As Jacob V. Joyce says, 'I really hope that the future shocks us, you know? I hope it shocks us in positive ways. I hope that the next generation of people are better.'

We remain hopeful that a better future is possible. Scattered across the world, people from marginalised communities have already come together and begun to build a future that cultivates safety over violence; our conversations with activists across different social movements are testament to this fact. So, despite the colossal task at hand, we cling to the abolitionist imagination and choose to follow the radical praxis of the revolutionaries that came before us and that stand with us today.

This is not a work for theorists. This framing and analysis must be applied in our daily lives. The rest of this work will explore how we practise abolitionist anti-violence work today, holding in mind a vision of transformative justice.

I.

LEARNING AND UNLEARNING

Even when we try to create our own spaces—our own little worlds inside this violent one—the violence tends to seep in. We end up recreating systems that exclude, isolate and silence. We hold other individuals and groups to a high standard and yet struggle to commit to the reflection that will help us to unlearn logics of violence and reach that standard ourselves. We often find ourselves recreating the cultural ideals of white supremacy through perfectionism, overworking and individualising harm. If we learn to practise our values of transformative justice in everything we do, applying these principles even when it comes to smaller instances of hurt and conflict, we will find ourselves much better equipped to approach more impactful, painful situations.

Learning can be a difficult process. Unlearning things we thought we understood about the world and facing how we have hurt others can be long and painful. We all have ways in which we protect ourselves from uncomfortable truths. Some of us like to make a joke or downplay the harm, some catastrophise and fall into a pit of self-loathing, and some bury our heads in books. Some of us decide to shift blame or attention, and some intimidate others until they stop challenging us. We need to accept that we are capable of making mistakes. If we can identify what our go-to tools are for defending ourselves—perhaps by chatting to people close to us about what they have noticed about the ways we handle conflict—and give ourselves some compassion for why we may have developed self-defensive mechanisms in the first place, we can then begin to learn to soften and take feedback with gratitude, rather than closing ourselves off and shielding ourselves from transformation.

For so many of us, the first site where we are exposed to violence is within our families. We might be subjected to or witness abuse, face the threat or experience of homelessness, or be harmed by queerphobic and ableist dynamics. We are taught to hold a kind of loyalty to our family members, even when they might hurt us. Often, we are dependent on our family network for shelter or support, creating a lack of accountability for people who are being violent. It is important to recognise that even someone who experiences many layers of oppression and hardship in their life might one day find themself with power over someone, and that person might be a child. We owe it to future generations to build accountability into our communities and to connect with new and old structures of 'family' outside of the nuclear, patriarchal unit.

Growing up, we can learn harmful habits and approaches in how to handle conflict. We are taught that the 'responsible' thing to do is to outsource our issues, whether to an older sibling, a parent, a church elder, a teacher or the police. Then, we see how that plays out—through punishment, separation and more harm. We live with the contradiction that when we ask for help, we might have to prove we're not the one that did something wrong. The work of abolitionists has emerged from this contradiction, since we know that existing avenues for support cause harm more often than not. So, we learn to improvise.

Abolitionist work is by and for marginalised people who have experienced violence, including child sexual abuse, sexual violence as adults and assault by police. We place those traumas at the centre of our analysis of violence, a tool of state control that we replicate in our everyday relationships. While theory can seem daunting, we have to learn how to apply our experience within a political framework. This political education should be done collectively, with the space for us to learn from each other and grow together. During the pandemic, we witnessed many abolitionist and radical reading groups emerge, such as Trans Abolitionist Futures and poc a dot reading group. Learning doesn't have to be inaccessible or done in isolation—it can be a way for us to gather lessons from our ancestors and map pathways to liberation. As well as public libraries, there are already hundreds of online resources such as Z-Library that provide free access to a wide range of radical texts.

The process of learning and unlearning can be challenging, but it is liberating too.

2.

SELF-ACCOUNTABILITY

Our ability to recognise when we are wrong, apologise and change our actions is a skill that is learnt. How we do this is dependent on many factors, including our lived identities and the expectations that family, friends and teachers have had of us since we were children.

Before we can get to a point of confidently and skilfully supporting others to be accountable for their actions, we need to reflect on what we ourselves do when we have crossed someone's boundary or hurt them in some way. It's always much easier to see the harm that others have inflicted on us than to see where we've messed up in our relationships. As explored in previous chapters, a key component of accountability is unpicking the idea of a 'good' or 'bad' person. Once we adopt the radical idea that everyone is deserving of having their basic needs met, whether food and shelter, or care and love, we can see that admitting to our flaws and owning up when we've hurt someone doesn't mean we become a 'bad person' who is undeserving of receiving support.

Reading these ideas might bring up a range of feelings. We grow up expecting to be shamed, excluded and isolated when we make a mistake. These early experiences mean that when someone tells us that we have harmed them, we perceive their words as a rejection or a threat. Our fight/flight/freeze/fawn response is triggered, because being called out makes us fearful. As we have learned through our exploration of the schooling system, punishment or the threat of punishment is often one of our first lessons. The kinds of punishments that we are vulnerable to might differ, but this disciplinary approach has instilled a strong sense of shame in us all.

Our position and experiences in society feed into how we are perceived, and in turn how we perceive ourselves. Who is considered harmful? Or dangerous? Who gets to be a victim? Who feels powerful enough to demand what they need, to speak up about harm they have faced? Who will be listened to when they speak up?

To try to prevent harm from escalating and to be proactive before harm happens, let's think about what we can do to help people feel comfortable to express themselves around us. We must actively seek meaningful feedback from people we care about and make time for deep conversations about our mistakes. It takes work to recognise our own boundaries and what we want to give and receive in relationships. When we are taught that there is a scarcity of resources and care, it's hard to honour the truth that our boundaries will not be the same as someone else's. If we approach our relationships with curiosity, we can engage with conflict and different needs as means to grow together, or as tools to work out that a relationship has run its course.

In our work supporting people to hold themselves to account after they have caused harm to people we love, understanding the differences between shame and guilt has proven essential. Sometimes it is necessary that we feel guilty about harm we have caused to someone else. But shame takes us to a place where we feel worthless and unable to believe we can make better choices. Guilt is about actions we have taken or choices we have made, which we can take responsibility for. Shame lets us surrender control of that responsibility.

One skill that many of us struggle with but that is a fundamental step towards accountability is apologising when we have caused someone harm or broken their trust. In these situations, it helps to ask people close to you who have not been harmed by your actions to support you to process your feelings and to work through your intentions and the impacts of the harm you caused. This way, you will find it easier to be in a good headspace to enter into dialogue with the person you harmed and to bring a meaningful apology to that conversation, instead of talking to them about how difficult everything has been for you. This practice is called 'dumping out, instead of in'.

We've learnt from Daria, a transformative justice practitioner who launched the Accountability Mapping online course, that somatic practices can be helpful to recentre ourselves when we're stuck swinging from under-accountability to over-accountability, from 'I didn't do anything, you're just too sensitive!' to 'I'm the worst person in the world!' Neither of these responses allows us to show up for the other person and be responsible for our actions.

The Bay Area Transformative Justice Collective has done brilliant work in helping us to understand how to make a full apology that shows we really are taking accountability for what we have done. Rather than providing a script for apologies, we encourage you to reflect on what has felt meaningful to you in the past when you have been harmed and to ask people close to you about what has been meaningful for them. For example, the actual words, 'I'm sorry,' may not be the most important part of an apology for everyone, but there are other ways to acknowledge and repair the harm. Some important aspects of apologising can be naming the actions or choices that you made that impacted the other person, showing that you understand why they were harmful, and making a commitment not to cause that harm again.

Be genuine in your apologies, don't put them off, and don't expect forgiveness or for your relationship to be repaired as a result. Ask if it's helpful to be forthcoming with options and ideas of ways to rebuild trust. Leave the conversation open, so it can be ongoing.

Within accountability processes and situations of relationship repair (conflicts where breaches of trust may have happened on multiple sides), it is important that we feel empowered to process the harm we have caused and to ask questions with the expectation that we will always treated as a whole person. If we work to repair harm and heal our relationships, we will hopefully be in a position to understand and gladly accept the consequences of our actions. New boundaries might be put in place that could shift as trust is rebuilt, and it is important to see this as an opportunity to respect those around us. Being accountable relies on us seriously considering how harm impacts our relationships, and finding ways to be transparent, considerate and sensitive in how we carry our experiences with us.

We are all capable of harm. Some of us are more likely to be supported than others—either when we experience harm or when we cause harm—which provides us with protection, a safety net or an escape. As we think about how to hold ourselves to account, we can reflect on who and what in our community supports us to do that.

To end this section, we extend an invitation to reflect on the following questions on power, defensiveness and taking responsibility.

- Where and how do you hold power in your life? (e.g. as a parent or a teacher, through age, race and gender)
- How are you affirming those around you?
- How are you making clear to others that you are open to feedback?
- Think of a time when you caused harm and didn't apologise or repair the relationship as well as you wish you had. What were your fears around taking accountability?
- How does being challenged make you feel?

- How do you feel when someone's boundary is different from your own?
- What are your tools for protecting yourself?
- How will you make sure to carve out time and space to address harm and support people around you?
- What has stopped you from being able to rebuild trust with someone you have harmed in the past?
- How can you communicate to others in an honest and sensitive way about harm you have caused in the past?
- How will you speak about the harm with people close to you and with new friends, partners, colleagues and comrades?

3.

TRANSFORMATIVE JUSTICE IN PRACTICE

Throughout this book, we have explored some of the many ways in which the principles of criminal justice are integrated into our everyday responses to conflict and violence. Against the carceral state, we believe, as Assata Shakur taught us, that if we desire freedom, we must embody it in everything we are and do.

In the world we live in now, we wait for harm to happen and let the state react with punishment. The criminal justice system does not provide support for survivors of violence and does nothing to address the circumstances that led to that violence. We must instead do what we can to prevent harm, and this requires us to recognise the behaviours that facilitate it, including those in which we participate ourselves.

As we move towards transformation, we hold the following goals in mind as the vision we are building towards:

- Safety, agency and healing for survivors
- Individual accountability and changes in perspective and behaviour for those who cause harm
- Collective accountability for the community's role in enabling harm

- Transformation of the social and material conditions that allow abuse to happen
- Liberation from all intergenerational legacies of violence and imperialism

We commit to the values of curiosity, because we have so much to learn; compassion, because we all must heal; and creativity, because we can build something new. Inspired by Generation Five in their mission to end child sexual abuse in five generations, we centre the following principles:

- Safety—the struggle against violence is at the heart of this work; liberation hinges on our safety at home, on the street and from state violence.
- Reclaiming Power—ending domination, coercive control and exploitation; building collective power.
- Accountability—the transformative power of holding ourselves individually and collectively responsible for our actions, our choices and the systems we uphold.
- Collective Action—abuse is enabled by isolation; only by working together can we take action to find justice for survivors and transform our conditions.
- Honouring Diversity—responding to violence in alignment with the specificities of culture, geographical region and historical context; there is no one recipe for this work.
- Sustainability—developing practices that last and can be repeated; understanding that transformation takes time; avoiding burnout by being clear about our limitations and expectations.

As we navigate the complexities of human relationships and power in our everyday lives, these values and guiding principles keep us facing in the direction of justice and love.

'Community' is trending; we've even seen the term co-opted

by the state with 'community custody units' in women's prisons. Your community, as far as we're concerned, is what you believe it to be—your people who see you through the good times and the bad. The first community that we become part of is the one that we are raised in: our families and their networks, including all the aunties and uncles that we're not sure whether we're actually related to. These early relationships are where we practise and learn how to give and receive love, support and feedback on our behaviour, so we can recognise when we mess up and make amends. For those of us who grew up among people who didn't support us, or who abused us, it can be much harder to learn how to build communities where we feel safe, and to trust them to hold us.

Some of us identify our community as being within a village, town, city or country; some of us don't, though we all exist in some form of relationship with those physically nearby. As we get older, we start building our own communities, often with school friends and neighbours, and sometimes around shared hobbies and interests, like football or anime. Identity-based communities also exist, such as those around race/ethnicity, sexuality and gender, especially for groups who are oppressed by the status quo. While white nationalists exist, most white people wouldn't identify themselves as being part of the 'white community' in the way that Black people might identify themselves as being part of a Black diaspora community.

By building relationships with members of our community, knowing whom to turn to in the face of harm and making use of the skills we already have, we can reduce our engagement with the police. If people in your community find themselves targeted by the police, what can you do to minimise those interactions? For example, some of our comrades in Houston, Texas, where police frequently use the excuse of broken taillights to harass and harm Black people, told us that a mechanic fixed everyone's taillights at the request of some community members.

As the pandemic has highlighted, we need each other. During a national lockdown, the UK government belatedly responded to the mental health crises suffered by single parents and those living alone by allowing them to form 'bubbles' with another household for emotional and physical support. The Bay Area Transformative Justice Collective, based in Oakland, California (occupied Ohlone land), came up with 'pods' as a tool to speak specifically about people in your life with whom you can engage in transformative justice work, whether that's the language you would use for it or not. These are the people you can call on to help you if you are in a crisis or unsafe. Your 'pod' also involves the people who would support you to be accountable if you hurt someone else.

To map your support pod, reflect on the following questions and lay out your responses. Don't worry if there are gaps at first, as you can work on building up your pod over time.

- Who could you rely on to support you if you were experiencing violence? Who could give you material support, like housing, food and travel money? Who could give you emotional support?
- Who could help you to reflect on your behaviour if you caused harm?
- Who do these people rely on for support? (Each person needs their own pod!)
- Who could be in your pod if you built a stronger relationship with them?
- What resources can you access, e.g. spare rooms, therapists, community groups and medical skills?

4.

COMMUNITY ACCOUNTABILITY

Transformative justice is about looking for ways to prevent, intervene in and address harm within our communities without relying on police or the state. Community accountability is a strategy within transformative justice to address violence when it happens around us. Most of the time, when people call the police, it is because they have a need that they believe only the police can meet. This could be a need to immediately remove someone who is being violent from an environment where they could cause harm, or it could be a need to recover a lost item. What if we used other, more effective, less harmful options to resolve these problems?

In British and Western culture, we hear accountability framed as how we 'hold someone to account'. Generally, this involves punishment, isolation from others and our needs not being met. We associate being held to account by others with being shamed. The practice of transformative justice requires us to look critically at the power dynamics involved in this approach, the coercive nature of 'making someone be accountable', and the way we become judge, jury and executioner in such a framework. Rather than holding others to account, the focus in transformative justice is to support people to take responsibility for themselves.

After running workshops with communities across the UK, we have seen how difficult it is to escape from the simplistic roles of victim, villain and hero. In this model, known as the Karpman drama triangle, there is a victim who has been harmed, is disempowered and feels hopeless; a villain who has caused harm, avoids blame and is punished; and a hero who swoops in to take care of people without being asked. In situations of conflict, we tend to bounce around between these roles, instead of finding a more nuanced place of recognition, accountability and support.

Speaking up about abuse within tight-knit communities is often terrifying. Our culture has normalised victim-blaming and prioritises the protection of the powerful over healing for survivors. The language we have to describe our relationships to people that have hurt us is very limited. We sometimes find that others seek to shove us into a narrative of victimhood, or accuse us of condemning people in our community as irredeemable when we are open about how their behaviour has affected us. This supports neither the healing of someone who's been hurt, nor the wider community transformation that is needed to prevent harm.

Believe survivors. When there are so many barriers to naming violence, if a person chooses to tell us about harm they have experienced, we have a major responsibility to show them it was the right choice to trust us. If we don't, we risk compounding their trauma and invalidating them, making them less likely to speak about their experience with anyone else. Be affirming of the person who has experienced harm; listen to them and let them know that you believe them. Ask them what they need and who else they want to involve so you can make a plan of support.

When power is centralised among one or a few people, we find serious cases of harm. We've worked with people experiencing harm in the family, the entertainment industry, parliament, business, hospitality, charities, churches, sports, schools and universities. Hierarchy enables abuse, and individualising the harm that is caused by one person without deconstructing the broader context that facilitated the harm will only allow abuse to continue.

Social media has warped our understanding of 'accountability'. We demand that celebrities and influencers make public apologies, which appear as screenshots of their Notes app if they really mean it. But this isn't really accountability when we have no idea if anything has changed behind the public persona. You can't be accountable to a million strangers that follow you online—accountability requires consent and active participation. And while conservatives have fuelled a moral panic about the idea of 'cancel culture', because people in power aren't used to getting feedback from the masses, in actuality, Black and queer people are the ones who bear the disproportionate wrath of the internet. We need to consider what will shift conditions and provide relief for survivors, rather than seeking emotion-fuelled mob justice.

We live in a society where it feels easier to exile someone than to deal with the messiness of addressing our problems. Much of British culture is passive-aggressive and revolves around the meaningless goal of appearing 'nice'. As a result, we often avoid conflict with our neighbours and friends, because conflict is seen as aggression, deemed to be a lower-class trait. But not all conflict is bad, and middle-class politeness can be just as controlling and harmful, papering over the structural issues that divide our communities. Sitting with the messiness of human emotions is essential for us to truly be in community with each other, while conflict is a necessary aspect of shifting power and transforming behaviour. We all need to be willing to be challenged.

If you see someone being harassed or abused in public, intervening is an important way to support them while also disrupting a culture that normally leaves such acts unchallenged. You may have done this for your friends before—when someone is dancing too close to your friend in the club, have you ever 'danced them out the way'? Or have you swapped seats on the bus to help your friend to get away from someone? If we extend this responsibility to strangers, we will all feel a little less alone. We start to send the message that harmful behaviour is unacceptable. Our top tip is to turn your attention from thinking about how to confront the person posing a threat, and instead to focus on the needs and agency of the person being harassed. That way, you're less likely to escalate the situation, and you can get creative.

Bystander intervention doesn't just have to be on the street or on public transport. When our friend Maya heard her neighbour being abused next door, she gradually befriended the person as they crossed paths every few days in the corridor. One night, when things with her neighbour's partner escalated to life-threatening levels, a group of neighbours intervened before the police were called. Maya opened her home to this survivor for a few days until they were able to source further support.

The criminal justice system provides a one-size-fits-all approach to any and all harm, but true accountability is as messy and nuanced as the people involved. There is no ready-made response to harm; we have to approach each situation with care and intention. In most instances of harm, people end up doing nothing rather than calling the police. If we start by saying, 'We're going to do *something* about this,' it motivates us to get creative.

We found that we have already developed an abundance of skills for community accountability simply through our experiences of surviving in the world. Each of us has skills we can bring to our communities; some of us can offer care work, some of us organise to tear down carceral institutions, some of us have financial resources to redistribute, and some of us are good at crafting useful things with power tools. The important point is that we all have a role to play within our community, and it is only when we come together with the mindset that no one is disposable that we can envision our collective liberation.

Questions to explore

- How do you support your friends to reflect on their actions when they've hurt someone or have done something out of alignment with their values?
- Who facilitates the conflict work in your communities?
- Think of a time you felt the need to call the police. Can you identify what you needed in that moment? How else could have you been supported by those around you to get what you needed?
- How are people being targeted by the state in your community?
- How might your community be targeted if you begin engaging in transformative justice and community accountability?

5.

JOY AND HEALING

We need to divest from systems of punishment and redirect our energy and resources into healing our communities and our planet.

So much of British culture is built around suffering and then wanting others to suffer like we did. We say, enough! Our liberation demands joy—a joy that fosters healing and that we share with our communities. The everyday violence of living within the prison industrial complex is memorialised in our bodies and passed down generations through our very DNA, but joy and healing can be our remedy. Our ancestors cultivated moments of joy as a form of resistance, and it is this legacy that we seek to embody.

True self-care is found in the abolitionist vision that keeps us alive and well in our communities. We cannot sustain ourselves or each other if we are completely burned out or so close to the edge that we have no space for compassion. Our lives matter, and so we must do what we can to look after our health. Protecting our communities from the pain and suffering inflicted on us by the state means that we must treat each other with the care and kindness that we all deserve. We need to stop punishing and policing ourselves and each other. A better future is possible.

Angela Davis tells us to practise radical self-care in order to 'bring our entire selves into the movement'. Part of building an abolitionist movement is the practice of self-love, holistic living and sustainable living. Alchemy, herbalism and rootwork can reconnect us with the land and with the food we eat. Reiki, meditation, yoga and other forms of grounding can provide us with the mental and emotional space to prevent harm and heal from trauma. Our vision is about building communities filled to the brim with love that transcends politeness, with the goal of eliminating violence and promoting unity.

Healing justice

Healing justice is a framework for recognising, processing and healing the impacts of lived and intergenerational trauma on our bodies, minds and spirits. Healing justice collectives by survivors and oppressed people have formed in communities across the globe to create spaces to engage with healing practices. Rather than being miserable most of the time, we have to recognise that we are all entitled to pleasure. Our bodies are hardwired for pleasure, not suffering. We know this because study after study shows us that the more stress in our lives, the more likely we are to pick up viruses and develop autoimmune diseases—suffering makes our bodies sick. Abolition calls on us to recognise the ways oppressive systems harm us, heal those wounds and transform our society into a more nurturing and compassionate one.

Collective grieving

The Covid-19 pandemic has opened up space for discussions about how exhausting the conditions that we live under are. These circumstances invite us to resist the individualisation of grief, poverty and suffering and to find new collective responses and strategies for healing. Throughout the pandemic, our current system hasn't given us time to grieve in our communities, care for ourselves, or celebrate together the legacies of the people we have lost. Instead, we have been hounded by bailiffs and bill collectors and have sometimes gone without food.

But in 2020, abolition offered a glimmer of hope, when mutual aid initiatives and grief support groups sprung up around the country. Some groups were set up to support people grieving loved ones who had died from Covid, while others facilitated community healing, such as the circles run by Healing Justice London for Black folks grieving during the Black Lives Matter protests. These spaces give us a way to reconnect with our ancestral mourning practices. The loneliness of grief often feels overwhelming, but having space to feel our way through these moments collectively paves the way for our joy. How do you grieve? What would it look like to grieve with others?

Building sustainable and nourishing political movements

There is a lot of work to be done, and we need to pace ourselves. We must remember that we are so much more than the trauma we endure. Ask yourself what brings you joy, who do you live for, what keeps you alive? These are answers that we should use to centre ourselves. Our movements are much more successful when we have fun with people we genuinely love and care about. When we laugh together and build warm, nourishing relationships, it makes us want to take responsibility for each other's wellbeing.

Building sustainable movements also means that we must know when to tear down the structures that we have built, so we can continue to form new bricks to replace the old.

Joy and resistance

In centring joy in our movements, we once again pay homage to the revolutionary work of Claudia Jones, who set up Notting Hill Carnival as a bold response to the racist violence and exclusion experienced by Caribbean people in the UK. Notting Hill Carnival is one of the biggest, most colourful street festivals in Europe. Always a celebration, it is an example of joy as resistance and the power of dance and music as a radical form of protest. Every year, Notting Hill Carnival is met with heavy police presence—despite arrest rates from 2016 to 2019 being almost identical to Glastonbury Festival when the number of attendees is taken into account—but this does not deter us.

Imagination, rest and creativity

Prisons uphold an extractive system that exploits the labour of racialised, impoverished people. The system is built on the myth of scarcity and competition; it discards people at the margins (who cannot or do not want to be exploited for their labour) and tells them that they are lazy and invaluable. These are lies. There are enough resources for us all to thrive.

Abolition is a creative project; it invites us to come up with new and innovative ways to support each other without relying on the violent state. We cannot underestimate the transformative power of rest, play, joy and healing, which are not frivolous activities but rather are essential to our liberation.

Our holistic wellbeing is required for the longevity of our movements. We need to be supported, healthy, nurtured, protected and safe; only then can we show up for each other and take on the system that is oppressing us.

We can't get through this alone. Our community is not just for support; it's who makes us laugh, who shares meals with us, who dances with us around the living room. The joy of being yourself, tasting freedom with your chosen family in a safe space, listening to music and creating art, dancing and practising movement work in order to free our bodies and minds, eating good food in comfortable spaces and dreaming together are all part of our revolutionary work. Our politics—and this book—would never have come to be if not for the joy of these revolutionary friendships.

REFLECTIONS

The work of abolition is deeply personal to us. This was a project of love—love for the movement and for our communities. Even though our collective is built around care and emotional vulnerability, we struggled with this project, spiralling through shame and perfectionism drummed into us by family, schools and universities. Working collaboratively has given us the courage and protection to produce imperfect, opinionated, principled work. We're still growing, and we're growing together.

There is so much more we could explore when it comes to the state's use of criminalisation, coercion and surveillance as tools to maintain control and oppression. Nonetheless, we hope this book provides a framework for blossoming abolitionists to get involved in whichever ways call to them. We learned so much about how much we don't know through this project, and we are excited to continue our learning.

To everyone who supported, contributed to and read this work—thank you.

GLOSSARY

Prison abolition: The dismantling of all social, political and economic institutions that sustain systems of prisons and policing. Abolition is imagining a world full of shared abundance, human dignity, safety, justice and freedom.

Prison industrial complex/carceral state: We use these terms interchangeably to refer not just to prisons, police, courts, detention centres and mental health detention, but also to the interconnectedness of the state with private companies that profit and benefit from imprisonment and securitisation.

Transformative justice: A set of practices for responding to harm that rejects policing, prisons and punishment, instead centring intervention in violence happening within our communities, support for people experiencing violence, understanding the community's role in enabling harm, and taking collective responsibility for changing the conditions that allowed harm to occur.

Community accountability: A strategy within transformative justice to address harm within a community, especially sexual violence and child abuse. It centres survivor support and accountability both for the individual who caused harm and the community that enabled it.

Imperialism: The exercise of state power to influence, control or dominate for the purpose of expanding the sphere of the state's economic and political control.

Colonialism/colonisation: The practice of territorial expansion through seizure of land and domination over colonised people, for the purpose of bringing economic and political benefit to the colonising country.

Settler colonialism: A form of colonisation that aims to replace the existing indigenous population with the colonisers, usually through genocide and displacement.

Globalisation: The increasing interconnectedness of the world's economies through financial deregulation, technological advances and the global exchange of cheap goods and labour, leaving in its wake dwindling economic, educational and social support opportunities for working-class communities.

Securitisation: The process by which a state turns social and political issues into matters concerning 'security', thus justifying increased state violence.

Patriarchy: A political-social system in which men dominate and take superiority over all other genders. Patriarchal domination is maintained through many forms of psychological and physical violence.

White supremacy: The political, economic and social domination of whiteness, maintained through the subjugation, dehumanisation and systemic oppression of Black people, people of colour and racialised people.

Racial capitalism: An economic system that prioritises the accumulation of money for wealthy individuals and corporations over the wellbeing of the working classes; under this system, the Global North extracts labour and resources from the Global South as justified by processes of racialisation.

LIST OF ORGANISATIONS

Sisters Uncut: sistersuncut.org

Critical Resistance: criticalresistance.org

Bay Area Transformative Justice Collective: batjc.wordpress.com

Survived and Punished: survivedandpunished.org

Generation Five: generationfive.org

INCITE!: incite-national.org

Combahee River Collective: combaheerivercollective.weebly.com/the-combahee-river-collective-statement.html

Community Action on Prison Expansion: cape-campaign.org

Smash IPP: smashipp.org.uk

Joint Enterprise Not Guilty by Association: jointenterprise.co

London Campaign Against Police and State Violence: lcapsv.net

Police Spies Out of Lives: policespiesoutoflives.org.uk

Spycops campaign: spycops.co.uk

United Families & Friends Campaign: uffcampaign.org

Campaign Against Arms Trade: caat.org.uk

Palestine Action: palestineaction.org

Anti-Raids Network: antiraids.net/about

Fight Toxic Prisons: fighttoxicprisons.wordpress.com

Prison Ecology Project: nationinside.org/campaign/prison-ecology-project

Project LETS: projectlets.org

Land In Our Names: landinournames.community

QueerCare: queercare.network

Together With Migrant Children: togethermigrantchildren.org.uk

Sins Invalid: sinsinvalid.org

UK Mutual Aid: facebook.com/groups/292963391332421

Decolonising Contraception: decolonisingcontraception.com

Dope Black Dads: dopeblackdads.com

Northern Police Monitoring Group: npolicemonitor.co.uk

Kids of Colour: kidsofcolour.com

No More Exclusions: nomoreexclusions.com

ICFree: twitter.com/icfreeuk

4Front Project: 4frontproject.org

Exist Loudly: twitter.com/existloudlyuk

Prisoner Solidarity Network: prisonersolidarity.wixsite.com/psnldn

Books Beyond Bars UK: beyond-bars.org

Bent Bars Project: bentbarsproject.org

Race & Health: raceandhealth.org

Child Poverty Action Group: cpag.org.uk

Corporate Watch: corporatewatch.org

Antiuniversity Now: antiuniversity.org

Good Night Out: goodnightoutcampaign.org

National Food Service Bristol: nationalfoodservicebristol.uk

Rose Hill Community Larder: mcsoxford.org/about-us/partnerships/community-larder

OLIO: olioex.com

LIST OF ORGANISATIONS

London Renters Union: londonrentersunion.org

Crossroads Women's Centre: crossroadswomen.net

Sex Worker Advocacy and Resistance Movement: swarmcollective.org

English Collective of Prostitutes: prostitutescollective.net

Inquest: inquest.org.uk

SUGGESTED READING

Akala, *Natives: Race and Class in the Ruins of Empire*, London: Two Roads, 2019.

Andaiye, ed. Alissa Trotz, *The Point is to Change the World: Selected Writings of Andaiye*, London: Pluto Press, 2020.

Boyce Davies, Carole, *Left of Karl Marx: The Political Life of Black Communist Claudia Jones*, Durham, NC: Duke University Press, 2008.

Boyce Davies, Carole, *Claudia Jones: Beyond Containment*, Banbury, Oxfordshire: Ayebia Clarke Publishing, 2010.

brown, adrienne maree, *Emergent Strategy: Shaping Change, Changing Worlds*, Chicago, IL: AK Press, 2017.

Cowan, Leah, *Border Nation: A Story of Migration*, London: Pluto Press, 2020.

Davies, James, *Cracked: Why Psychiatry is Doing More Harm Than Good*, London: Icon Books, 2013.

Davis, Angela Y., *Women, Race & Class*, New York: Random House, 1981.

Davis, Angela Y., *Are Prison Obsolete?*, New York: Seven Stories Press, 2003.

Davis, Angela Y., *Freedom Is a Constant Struggle: Ferguson, Palestine and the Foundations of a Movement*, Chicago, IL: Haymarket Books, 2015.

de Noronha, Luke, *Deporting Black Britons: Portraits of Deportation to Jamaica*, Manchester: Manchester University Press, 2020.

Dixon, Ejeris & Leah Lakshmi Piepzna-Samarasinha (eds), *Beyond Survival: Strategies and Stories from the Transformative Justice Movement*, Chicago, IL: AK Press, 2020.

Dysophia, 'What About the Rapists?: Anarchist Approaches to Crime and Justice', 2014, https://dysophia.org.uk/wp-content/uploads/2014/09/Dys5-WhatAboutTheRapistsWeb2.pdf.

Elliott-Cooper, Adam, *Black Resistance to British Policing*, Manchester: Manchester University Press, 2021.

Faye, Shon, *The Transgender Issue: An Argument for Justice*, London: Penguin, 2021.

Gay, Roxane, *Not That Bad: Dispatches from Rape Culture*, London: Atlantic Books, 2018.

Haines, Staci, *The Politics of Trauma: Somatics, Healing, and Social Justice*, Berkeley, CA: North Atlantic Books, 2019.

hooks, bell, *All About Love: New Visions*, New York: Harper, 2000.

James, C.L.R., *The Black Jacobins: Toussaint L'Ouverture and the San Domingo Revolution*, London: Secker & Warburg, 1938.

Kaba, Mariame, *We Do This 'Til We Free Us: Abolitionist Organizing and Transforming Justice*, Chicago, IL: Haymarket Books, 2021.

Levins Morales, Aurora, *Medicine Stories: Essays for Radicals*, Durham, NC: Duke University Press, 2019.

Olufemi, Lola, *Feminism, Interrupted: Disrupting Power*, London: Pluto Press, 2020.

Piepzna-Samarasinha, Leah Lakshmi, *Care Work: Dreaming Disability Justice*, Vancouver, BC: Arsenal Pulp Press, 2018.

Richie, Beth E., *Arrested Justice: Black Women, Violence, and America's Prison Nation*, New York, NY: New York University Press, 2012.

Rodney, Walter, *How Europe Underdeveloped Africa*, London: Bogle-L'Ouverture Publications, 1972.

Russo, Ann, *Feminist Accountability: Disrupting Violence and Transforming Power*, New York, NY: New York University Press, 2018.

Shakur, Assata, *Assata: An Autobiography*, London: Zed Books, 1987.

Sivanandan, A., *Communities of Resistance*, London; New York: Verso Books, 1990.